BOTH SIDES OF PARADISE:

A MEMOIR

Bob Shults

[Copyright Page]

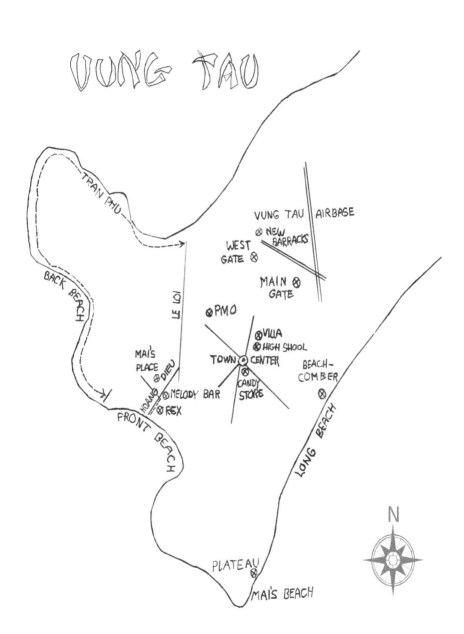

VUNG TAU

DEDICATION

To my wife Sherry without whom my world would stop turning, and to my daughter Robin and granddaughters, Ashley and Alex, in hopes they will finally understand the father and grandfather they have never really known.

SPECIAL THANKS

To my Pastor for empathizing with my need to narrate the first three quarters of this memoir from a less-than-Christian perspective. As he said, "It's all part of the journey."

"If we confess our sins, He is faithful and righteous to forgive us our sins and to cleanse us from all unrighteousness."

1 John 1:9

Table of Contents

PART ONE
Military

PART TWO
Civilian Life

FOREWORD

I spent three tours of duty in Vietnam as a Military Policeman and two years as an investigator (civilian) working for AAFES (Army Air Force Exchange Services). I'm fairly knowledgeable as to what really went on with the troops and what didn't. Not everyone served honorably and not everyone will give you the real story of their time in-country. Much is told of bravery and their "time in hell," but for most who served nothing could be further from the truth. For every one combat soldier there were nine or so in the rear supporting him, *i.e.*, clerks, motor pool, cooks, mechanics, etc., etc., etc. The list goes on and on.

I recently read a book by an MP that gets rave reviews on-line. He was so "brave" but the only problem is, he took every known incident involving Military Police combat that was known in Vietnam over several years and gave himself credit for it, all crammed into his one year tour of duty. Far too many Vietnam Vets claim the same thing.....their *time in hell*, when in fact many spent their one year in the confines of a base that they never left, perhaps only to visit a local house of ill repute while smoking a joint. Now on to Bob Shults and his memoir, "*Both Sides of Paradise.*"

If I didn't need sleep and my old eyes didn't dry out I would have read it in one sitting. Bob was an MP with the 560th MP Company stationed in Vung Tau, the R&R (rest and recuperation center) his entire one year tour of duty. Bob was essentially a beat cop. Most of us were, although there were certainly duties, such as convoy escorts, that put us in danger and even under attack.

There were lots of unrelated non-combat deaths and tragedies in Vietnam. Even an MP who gets mysteriously murdered, and then the FUBARs (Fouled Up Beyond All Repair). Bob tells these FUBARS, in which we ALL were involved, with a dry sense of humor. Bob, refreshingly so, is not afraid to self-denigrate (which should be a lesson to us all). Bob is able to convey the love/hate relationship that sometimes occurred between the Vietnamese and us, and he does it with all due respect.

Coming from a dysfunctional family (but with a strong loving mother) Bob relates this by telling his Vietnam story with flashbacks to his childhood. His writing is detailed (remembering many more details than I can in my old age) and keeps you interested.

Bob saw his share of blood, as most "cops" would, but after all that and when returning to the States the oft inexplicable impact of that year weighs on him....."I'd been happier in Vietnam." I went through the same thing. I called it "rambling." I just couldn't get my act together, wandered off, hitchhiked across the country, etc. Bob was the same, but he was married and had a child and things did not bode well resulting in him not seeing his daughter for decades while he dabbled in drugs and "living (his) life to the fullest."

But the epiphany comes, late in his life. It comes and Bob finds his footing and reason once more. Bob moves on and realizes there are choices in life. Yes, Vietnam lingers there, but no groveling in pity with a false claim of PTSD, he gets it together.

This is a fresh and REAL look at the average tour of duty for our men who served in Vietnam setting aside the horror that the actual combat troops and the smattering of violence others may have seen. He has told his story with dignity, TRUTH, injected with humor and a great deal of HONOR.

Jim Stewart
Author: *Angel from Vietnam*

PREFACE

If one hangs out with endurance cyclists long enough, the discussion eventually turns to their dream rides. Some say a stage of the Tour de France, maybe the Col du Galibier, others the infamous "RAGBRAI...the ride across Iowa," or even a coast-to-coast ride. But I always turn a few heads when I say Hanoi to Saigon in Vietnam. The inevitable question is "why in the world would you want to go back there?"

I've had contact with a lot of vets since the war and even the ones who want to return cannot adequately answer that question. I have heard it said it would be like visiting your own tombstone.

To me, my year in Vietnam is an old black and white photograph that I saw only once, and then, it was lost. A photo of a young kid full of spit and vinegar who thought he was invincible yet couldn't for all the world figure out how he managed to do some of the things he did, just because it was expected of him. A photo of a young Military Policeman who turned 21 over there and who could laugh so hard he almost fell out of a Jeep; yet be so frightened at times that he couldn't think straight...or at all.

Who would not want to find that old, faded, creased photo, focus in on it at arm's length, and look at it one more time before he leaves this world?

This Memoir is that black and white photograph.

"We have shared the incommunicable experience of war;

We have felt, we still feel, the passion of life to its top."

"In Our Youths, Our Hearts Were Touched With Fire"

The Soldier's Faith

--Oliver Wendell Holmes--

PART ONE
MILITARY

Chapter 1

MID-AUGUST 1966

The Korean was lying on the floor of the bar face down, legs splayed. One arm was under his body, the other was draped over a broken wooden chair. Sergeant Kim[1] was standing over him grinning at me.

It happened so fast, I felt the pain before I knew the cause. Kim nudged the seemingly unconscious ROK Marine on the knee with his nightstick. Lightning fast the guy shot to his feet, knocking over his chair and kicking at me, aiming for my groin. Missing, he splintered the corner of the cheap table he'd been sitting at. Formica slammed against the inside of my left thigh. Before I could move, the Marine was prone on the floor and Kim was standing over him with that white toothed grin of his.

"I tell you what, Sarge, you gotta be the fastest Korean in Vietnam."

"Least I faster than him," he said, still grinning, and pointing at the prostrate Marine.

EARLY OCTOBER 1965

My country was at war in Vietnam, but heroics had nothing to do with why I was standing in front of an Army recruiter. Boredom would be a better word. I had a good job with General Electric in Schenectady, New York, where I was born. I worked in the modular display department, putting my associate degree in advertising art and design to good use but I wanted to do more and see more before I settled down with a job near home.

The only times I'd ever been outside New York State were to travel by car with my mom and stepdad to Utah to visit my sister Jo and, before that, to the coast of Massachusetts with them and my favorite nephew "Bud." I figured the military could be the answer.

I went to the Navy recruiter first, thinking "*Join the Navy–See the World*," but their enlistment was four years. It was the same obligation with the Air Force and I certainly didn't want to be a Marine. I wasn't that bored! The only thing left was the Army with its 3-year hitch. I could have volunteered for the draft and gone in for two, which would have satisfied the "gypsy in my soul," but I didn't know that at the time, and a recruiter certainly wasn't going to say anything, because it wouldn't help him with his monthly quota.

Ironically, a few days after I signed the paper giving three years of my life to Uncle Sam and waiting for "further instructions," I received my draft notice. When I called the recruiter, he told me to just ignore it and show up at the recruitment center when I received the mailed orders.

---

[1] Some names have been changed.

A week later I got my letter telling me to report to Albany and bring nothing but toiletry articles and the clothes on my back, since the clothes I wore would be given to charity and I wouldn't need civilian wear for quite some time. My reporting date was October 18th.

Somehow, during that two weeks, both the people at my job as well as my family managed to put together going-away parties which was thoughtful, except one of the gifts was an electric razor and the first time my drill instructor (DI) saw me using it, he said that the next time I tried it, I'd be shaving with a bayonet.

Party at work:

Larry (a guy about my age and extremely glad he wasn't joining up) said, "Don't do anything I wouldn't do."

Marty (our workplace comedian), "Yeah, if you do, name it after Larry."

Mark (my closest friend at work and the one who set up the party) added, "Keep your head down."

Marty, "Yeah, not up some officer's butt."

My boss's advice was a little more enlightening, "I spent three years in the Army. Wouldn't want to do it again but it's something that'll always be with you." (At the time I didn't know just how prophetic that was.)

Family Party:

Brother Les: (eight years older than me and an Air Force veteran) suggested, "Be quiet in basic training, be invisible, it's the ones with the big mouths that get in trouble."

Brother Ed contributed, "Don't ever volunteer." Eddie helped me get the job at GE.

Brother-in-Law Harold, the family comedian, chimed in, "Why don't you just go to Canada and be done with it?"

~~~~~~

My physical in Albany was basically standing naked in front of military physicians with a lot of other embarrassed 17 to 20-year olds while bending over spreading our cheeks or, saying "ah" while choking on tongue depressors, or coughing while they handled our genitals.

"Turn your head, dipshit, he doesn't want any of your 'skanky' germs." This from one of two intimidating, yet impressive looking military policemen, not particularly enjoying their current duty assignments.

2

After we put on our civilian clothes for the last time, we pledged our Oath of Enlistment to the United States Army:

"I, Robert George Shults, do solemnly swear that I will support and defend the Constitution of the United States of America against all enemies, foreign and domestic; that I will bear true faith and allegiance to the same; and that I will obey the orders of the President of the United States and of the officers appointed over me, according to regulations and the Uniform Code of Military Justice so help me God."

What in the world had I gotten myself into?

We rode to New York City on a chartered Greyhound bus and transferred to a bus owned by the Army. It looked like a school bus, only green...a color we would come to know and love as O.D. or olive drab, (*as in dull or cheerless?*). Our destination was Fort Dix, New Jersey.

We arrived at the base around dusk to the sight of several surly looking sergeants dressed exactly alike in O.D. uniforms, also known as fatigues, and Smokey Bear hats. They wore the straps behind their heads, so the hats could be tipped forward to cover their eyes, unless the brim was close enough to touch your forehead while they screamed at you, which happened a lot.

"What are you smiling at, dipshit? Do I look funny to you? If you or any of these ladies so much as grin, I'll shove my boot so far up your ass your breath will smell like shoe polish for a month."

Yet you were not supposed to look them in the eyes, which was hard to do since their eyes were only five inches from yours.

They half-marched, half-shoved us to a long one-story building.

"You can move faster than that, lard ass."

Then they made us strip, again, so we could throw our civvies into laundry baskets. Then we were given a small slip of paper with our individual serial number and told to have it memorized by the time we got to the end of the long counter separating us from the soon-to-be tossed at us and quickly donned uniforms (O.D.) and to remember that number forever: *RA12740476.*

Everything we were now wearing was O.D. except a white T-shirt and boxer shorts. Carrying our two extra sets of fatigues, a web belt, brass buckle with a sliding brass bar to lock it into place (just like I had as a kid in Boy Scouts), six pairs of socks and, of course, a pair of combat boots – all in new Army-issued duffle bags.

We were marched/shoved to another long one-story building. This one was the mess hall. "Take all you want, but eat all you take." After chow we were marched (we began to realize that the quicker we learned to march, the less we were shoved), to a third long one-story building full of bunks.

We had all been through an exceptionally long and stressful day and fell asleep immediately. Unfortunately, we were awakened three hours later and marched back to the mess hall, not to eat, but to stand at parade rest in three rows along the full length of the building.

Once we all figured out what parade rest was, this sergeant, buzz cut and newly lit cigar sticking out of the corner of his mouth, appeared in an open window. Resting his burly tattooed forearms on the sill, the first thing he said in his gravelly southern accent was, "If at any time during my orientation some of you ladies think you're gonna faint, drop where you are and just lie there like a little pussy."

I assumed he was going to lead us on a tour of the post pointing out places of interest but was disappointed to learn that his *orientation* was to just stand in place and tell us about all the horrors we were going to endure for the next eight weeks.

Once I caught on, I didn't listen to too much of what he said since, sure enough, several of us "ladies" fainted and laid there like "little pussies." He even laughed when one guy collapsed face-first into the grass because his hands were still clasped at the small of his back in the just-learned parade rest position. The guy just laid there, not moving, as did several others that fainted with no one coming to their aid.

Then my sleepless night, my last day as a civilian, my long and stressful day on the 18th (ending with only three hours sleep and still no food yet that morning), caught up with me.

Fortunately, I was standing next to the railing attached to the steps leading to the door of the mess hall. As imperceptibly as possible, I shifted most of my weight off my feet to my left hip by leaning it against the railing.

The sergeant talked all the way through the length of his cigar until only about 70% of us remained standing when he dismissed us. At first, I was delighted; I passed my first "test" in the Army. But then the other 30% jumped up and fell into line like nothing happened, and I realized that they were the smarter ones since they had up to 20 minutes more sleep than the rest of us.

It's weird, but I don't remember when I received something as vital as dog tags. They were two pieces of tin about 1"x2" with letters and numbers pressed into them: last name, first name, middle initial, serial number, blood type, Social Security number and religion. Mine read "Protestant." Each had a hole in one end to slide onto a long keychain-type necklace.

They told us to never remove them. If you were killed in action, an officer was to take one to be turned into headquarters and the other would be jammed between your top and bottom front teeth, before you were zipped up in a black plastic bag (hence the term *tag'm and bag'm*).

They also told us to put our serial numbers in all our clothing, especially our boots, in case we died in an explosion, they could match up the correct body parts.

Chapter 2

BEGINNINGS

We were at the induction center one more day before we boarded an Army bus and went to another part of Fort Dix to start our basic training, where another group of sergeants in fatigues and Smokey Bear hats were waiting for us. They were our DIs for this eight-week ordeal, but the screaming was the same. The first shout aimed at me was, "Move your ass; you're big enough to eat that duffle bag."

We marched to our barracks, our platoon's home for the next eight weeks. It was yet another long building. Inside were bunks lined up on both sides with one end against the wall and the other pointed toward the aisle. Across the entire length of one end was the latrine: showers, sinks, mirrors, and toilets without any kind of privacy partitions. The first time I used the toilet, the guy next to me asked, "Do you know the Army way you're supposed to use toilet paper?"

"No."

Show and tell: "You take one square of toilet paper, find the center and tear it out, making a hole about the size of your index finger. You put the little piece aside and slide the square over your finger down to your knuckles. Then you stick your finger in your ass, (at this point the show and tell ended) moving it up and down while pressing your knuckles and the toilet paper against your cheeks. You remove your finger, flush the paper, and use the small piece to clean under your nail."

At 0500 hours every morning, we woke to the same sounds: our DI banging two trashcan lids together and shouting, "Drop your cocks and grab your socks. You got six minutes to make up your bunks and stand on top of your foot lockers." They did this to check our feet for calluses, blisters or toe jam. The significance of this became clearer as the weeks progressed. Then came, "Now get your asses to the latrine – shit, shower and shave." In less than 30 minutes, we'd all be in uniform ready for whatever training they had planned for that day.

A lot of it was physical training and a lot of physical training was running. After one five-mile jaunt before breakfast, I said, "My, that was fun."

Our DI: "Cute, Shults. Now drop, give me 20, and tell me if that's fun."

"Be quiet in basic training. Be invisible. It's the ones with big mouths that get in trouble."

With Brother Les' voice in my head and being exhausted, I was struggling after the first four push-ups. (And being 220 pounds at the time didn't help.) A couple of guys started snickering, so they had to drop and do 20 as well, then a few more laughed and it became sort of a domino effect. Soon the whole platoon was doing push-ups. Eventually, our DI said, "Screw it," and dropped down for 20 himself. So much for being "invisible."

"What's the spirit of the bayonet?" they shouted. Our response was "KILL! KILL! KILL!" as we thrust the bayonets several times into swaying canvas bags full of sawdust. *This was not a place for pacifists!*

We detached our bayonets from our M14s by the numbers since they were quite sharp.

1. Grab your rifle by the barrel with your right hand and rest the stock on the toe of your right boot.

2. Clasp the bayonet handle with your left hand and depress the release button with your right thumb.

3. Tilt the weapon away from your face.

4. Smartly jerk the bayonet off the rifle barrel and re-insert it into the sheath on your web belt.

There was one guy in our platoon (I'm sure every platoon had one), who always seemed to have trouble following orders or instructions. Not with obeying them, but rather, understanding them. This time it was forgetting number three and he stabbed himself through the corner of his mouth and out his cheek.

The first time someone called his rifle a gun, the whole platoon was made to stand in line, hold our rifles by the stock in our right hand and grab our crotch with our left, chanting,

> "This is my rifle,
> This is my gun,
> This is for shooting,
> This is for fun"

while lifting the appropriate hand on the appropriate word.

We didn't learn a lot of field first aid in basic because that was the job of the medics, but one thing stuck with me:

DI, "If you come across some poor bastard with his guts hanging out, do not, I repeat, do not, try to stuff everything back in. Just bandage it all in place and wait for medivac. Or else if you run into the guy some day and he opens his mouth to thank you, he's liable to shit in your face."

Rabbit hunting with my stepdad paid off at the target range. I was one of the first guys to cluster three rounds into an area the size of a quarter, so we received a two-day pass.

Having been born and raised in upstate New York, this wasn't my first time in the Big Apple, but I saw it now through different eyes. I was proud of my uniform and the glances we got from the civilians. This was before I was even aware of protests over the war.

However, a cab driver ripped us off when he griped about the size of our tip. I believe our uniforms screamed tourist. The neatest thing to me was the hotel we picked, for no reason other than it happened to be right across the street from a famous Italian restaurant that I had seen advertised in Schenectady.

~~~~~~

The point of the night-targeting range training was to learn to shoot others you could hardly see. Throughout that whole exercise, a verse kept coming back to me from a World War I song that my mom taught me:

> "I didn't raise my boy to be a soldier,
> I brought him up to be my pride and joy.
> Who dares to put a musket on his shoulder?
> To kill some other mother's darling boy?"

The night infiltration course was quite an adrenaline rush. We filed into a long trench about shoulder height. Then, like in every World War I movie I'd ever seen, at the sound of a whistle, we climbed out of the trench and low crawled 100 yards on our elbows under barbed wire; around, through or over various other debris; and past sandbag bunkers where they exploded satchel charges as we squirmed past, while M50 machine guns fired live rounds and tracers over our heads. We were told they were about four feet above our prone bodies. Judging from the tracers coming toward us, I'd say that was about right.

At the grenade range, we spent hours handling dummies before we got to throw live ones. The bayonet victim, or *Scarface* as he came to be known, lobbed his so short we heard sand and gravel hit the tin roof over our heads as we waited our turn.

Thanksgiving was a high point during basic training since we received permission to invite guests. My parents drove down from Schenectady (3½ hours) and brought my girlfriend. That was a mistake on their part since she and I spent most of their self-driven site-seeing tour of the base necking in the back seat of mom's car.

After Thanksgiving, during a quick-step drill exercise, out of the corner of my eye I saw our instructor talking to a couple of officers and shaking his head with, what appeared to be, disgust. He then climbed on a bench and made everyone gather around. "You sons-a-bitches can't even march but they're gonna make some of you military police...I'll be damned if I got no idea why." Then he started reading off a list. I was still chuckling over both his opinion of our marching abilities and his grammar when I heard my name.

As an enlistee, the recruiter said that sometime during basic training I would be able to choose my MOS (military occupational specialty). At that point I thought *Airborne*, because jumping out of an airplane seemed cool. After only one week of basic training, I realized that a soldier hanging in the air from a parachute made a very tempting target. Since then I hadn't had time to think about it.

Hearing the words, "military police," was like an epiphany. I forgot the fact that I didn't get to choose a MOS; and all I could think about was how sharp looking MP uniforms were. Either khakis, like the two guys at the Army recruiting center, or dress greens; both with white saucer cap and gloves and a green pistol lanyard and ascot, or in fatigues with a shiny black helmet liner. All sporting a black brassard (armband) with MP in white. And, best of all, a black Sam Browne belt with right shoulder cross strap for the khakis and dress greens or web garrison belt for fatigues. Both belt styles held handcuffs, an ammo pouch that carried two 7-round clips, a nasty-looking night stick and a deadly looking .45 caliber, model 1911, Colt automatic pistol.

Even as a kid, I loved uniforms. To me, one of the best things about Boy Scouts and Explorers were the uniforms. Only now I got to carry lethal weapons to boot!

The three whose names were called left drill instruction and were led to the administration building. We were asked if we had committed any felonies or misdemeanors or ever used illegal drugs, and then we filled out a lot of paperwork.

A few days later I was told I had received top secret security clearance, as opposed to the other two who received regular security clearance, which was mandatory for MPs. I don't know why they put me in the military police, let alone gave me such a high clearance. Apparently, they never found out about Bud and me being arrested in 1961. It was on a Saturday, May 20th, just five days before my 16th birthday, so I was still considered a juvenile and my records were sealed.

Throughout basic training I did my turns on guard duty, as fire guard and on KP, which consisted mostly of cleaning stoves and peeling potatoes. Having worked in fast food restaurants in high school, I knew that peeling machines existed, so I assumed the Army simply didn't want to discontinue one of its iconic kitchen duties.

We graduated mid-December. My folks did not come down, most likely because of my necking marathon over Thanksgiving. The highlight of the graduation for a lot of us was the look of horror from Scarface's parents when they saw a great mound of gauze and surgical tape from his mouth to his ear.

When we returned to the barracks for our last night of basic, we found several bottles of celebratory hard liquor. It was our DI's way of telling us we were no longer "little pussies." I'm told I did the low crawl across the room in just underwear, steel helmet and M14.

Chapter 3

PRAETORIAN GUARD

Our written orders said to show up at the MP academy in Fort Gordon, Georgia, on New Year's Eve. I guess I was the only one who read his orders: I welcomed 1966 alone, on a foot locker, in an empty barracks. Everyone else showed up on New Year's Day in various stages of hangovers.

Sergeants were no longer DIs, they were now our assistant platoon leaders. Sergeant Byrd was a 35-year old, 5'10", African-American career soldier with a baritone voice that was too much of a temptation not to try and mimic. He loved the Army and the military police. One could see it in his demeanor. We all felt he had a genuine desire to make us the best MPs we could be.

We loved the marching songs he'd lead us in:

> "Mama, mama, look at me.
> I'm gonna be a big MP.
> With my pistol and handcuffs,
> little bit of Judo to make me tough."

although a little morose at times:

> "If I die in a combat zone,
> box me up and send me home.
> Lay my pistol on my chest;
> tell my mom I did my best."

I guess MPs were supposed to be classier than the average grunt. In basic our DI taught us a lot saltier songs.

During a night orientation course, much to our surprise, Sergeant Byrd interrupted our training and marched the whole platoon back to our barracks. A team of doctors and nurses were waiting to examine us because Jim Samples, the guy who slept right below me, came down with spinal meningitis.

For the rest of the MP academy cycle, all the platoons were made to sleep "head to toe," an Army euphemism that meant heads above feet in the bunks, with the opposite arrangement for the bunks on either side. If we went to the Post's theater, we sat with an empty seat to the left and right – front and back. The Army takes communicable diseases very seriously. Jim Samples simply disappeared for the rest of the cycle.

Oddly, marching, like uniforms, appealed to my sense of order and, well, uniformity. Sergeant Byrd picked up on my enthusiasm for the former and let me lead the whole platoon through its paces. Shouting, "plaah-toon, colummmn right h'arch!" and having 100 uniformed military police cadets do exactly that was a real hoot.

Halfway through our eight weeks the whole platoon received a one-night pass. We quickly ascertained which Augusta, we pronounced it "Discusta," hotel contained the most circulating prostitutes. After all, wasn't that what a one-night pass was for?

Like many firsts in the military, this resulted in my first experience with a prostitute. With just a phone call to the main desk, four hours later my buddy and I opened the door for a woman who was around 10 years older than either of us. She made us take turns waiting in the bathroom while she entertained the other. She was quite attractive, except for her mangled hairdo and several runs in her stockings.

During basic training, with all its intensity and relentless rigidity, we all felt the need to cling to the thought of a sweetheart back home. I guess it helped to keep us grounded to the reality we were familiar with on the outside. Writing letters and especially receiving them from our ladies was the highlight of basic training. It made the whole thing more bearable. Another marching song:

> "Ain't no use in going home,
> Jody's got your gal and gone.
> Ain't no use in going back,
> Jody's got your Cadillac"

made us all fear the dreaded "Dear John" letter. I figured my relationship was secure, especially after Thanksgiving. That all changed in Georgia.

At the Academy there was still a lot of intense training ... from how to break up a bar fight to handling our .45's correctly. "Shults, you'd better take your hand off the top of that weapon or you're gonna lose a finger...that ain't no six shooter." But overall, we were treated with more patience and respect. I mean, we were to be the new praetorian guard. "The military is only as good as its police force."

Consequently, my need to be grounded, at least to a sweetheart on the outside, seemed less important. I stopped writing (and receiving) letters, until I got my "Dear John." Apparently, I still needed to feel grounded. I felt and acted like a six-year old who lost his favorite teddy bear.

Enter Sergeant Byrd. He did something there is no way in Hades would have happened in basic training. He noticed my distress and asked what was wrong. When I told him, he dismissed me from training that day and let me stay in his room in our barracks until I got over it.

That's what I did, but I kind of felt like...what was that phrase from the induction center? "A little pussy?" I guess I was over it by noon, but since I knew training that day was night stick tactics (we basically beat each other with clubs), I stayed in his room...I'm not stupid.

A week before we graduated, we were all gathered together to learn if we were going to Vietnam. If so, we would gct 30-days' leave. If not, we would have less than a week to get to our next duty station.

As each name of those headed for Vietnam was called, that person would let out a little yelp of pleasure. Each of us hoped the others would think it was because we were going to a war zone to fight for *freedom and the American way* but mostly it was for the 30-day leave.

Soon after, all those headed for Vietnam had to go to supply and exchange their white underwear for OD. I said "Gee, why are we turning in all our whites? So, we won't have anything to surrender with?" Nobody laughed.

 A portent of things to come: just before we left Georgia, two civilians robbed a liquor store and somehow ended up on-Post. When they tried to leave through the main gate, the MP on duty tried to stop and ID them. He was shot in the face. The military has a habit of naming places after people who have been killed. The main gate at Fort Gordon became McKenna Gate.

Chapter 4

HURRY UP AND WAIT

During leave my girlfriend and I made up, slept together, and broke up again. But that was the furthest thing from my mind.

It was dusk and the end of a 10,000-mile, 18-hour flight when we started circling Saigon Airport. We were still high enough to see jungle and billowing orange plumes of flame from Napalm, a highly flammable sticky jelly used in incendiary bombs consisting of gasoline thickened with special soaps. The plumes appeared to be only 10 or 15 miles from the city.

As I felt the tug of the jet engines slowing and watched that roiling orange glow, which in my mind was a good sign that someone was being burned alive, I realized there was a chance I actually might not survive Vietnam.

I needed to decide how I was going to handle that possibility. I decided either I would or wouldn't die. There was not much I could do about it at this point...short of desertion. This wasn't bravery, but more like resignation.

I did, however, make a promise to myself that if I made it back, I would live my life to its fullest, whatever that meant. I didn't give much thought to the existence of God, but I guess I felt that if He did exist, my good outweighed my bad. Nonetheless, that was when I decided to keep a small New Testament Gideon Bible in my helmet liner.

Our landing was quite abrupt and a little frightening because pilots learned early in the war to land and take off at steep angles to avoid ground fire.

It was a short ride from Saigon to Tan Son Nhut Air Base by Army bus. They put us up in the "transit barracks" to await our duty assignments and in-country orientation. At least we got to sit down for this one. It consisted mostly of color photographs of male genitalia infected with various kinds of venereal disease, ending with the admonition to always wear a prophylactic.

On my second day at the base I checked out the enlisted men's club. I spotted a guy with the crossed flintlock pistols insignia on his fatigue shirt, an MP. His chair was reversed, arms crossed on the chair back. I asked if I could sit, tapping my insignia. "Yeah," he said, nodding.

Judging by the number of opaque plastic cups in front of him, he'd been there a while. He said his tour was over and he'd be leaving country in the morning.

I told him I just found out that I was going to be posted with the Second Platoon of the 560th Military Police Company.

"No shit, man, that's my unit. I just left there! But the best part is the location, Vung Tau, man! It's an in-country R&R center. Except for maybe 'dust-off' and some 'conny' runs, it's all 'kick-ass and take names'." He was waving his beer around, dangerously close to spilling it.

I didn't know what he was talking about, something he picked up on right away.

"You might be asked to volunteer for 'dust-off'."

"What's that?"

"Door gunner on a medical chopper."

"Is that like...?"

"Manning a '60'."

"What's that?"

"An M60 machine gun you fire from the door of a "Huey."

"What...what's that?"

"It's a Bell UH-1 military helicopter; they go in and pick up the dead and wounded."

"Wait...what?" I asked, eyes focused on his animated plastic cup.

"Yeah, you only open fire if Charlie fires first because he's ignoring the big red cross on the door and nose."

"You mean a cross on the...wait, who's Charlie?"

"That's the enemy."

"Um."

"It's short for Victor Charlie, military phonetic alphabet for VC, that's short for Vietnamese Communist. 'Conny runs' mean armed convoy escort."

"But..."

"And 'kick-ass and take names' is regular police work...well...only in a war zone, where you deal with grizzled old merchant marines who carry every hand weapon known to man."

"You mean like...?"

"You know, saps, brass knuckles, Bowie knives," he interrupted, not for the first time, beer cup inching closer to me with every word. "But mostly it's drunken combat infantry guys just in from 'Indian Country.'"

"Is that?"

"The bush."

"You mean...?"

"Enemy territory."

I figured I better stick with this guy for as long as I could, if only to learn this entirely new vernacular he picked up in the town I was headed for.

That may have been a mistake. His next words were, "Listen, I want to celebrate going home, and you gotta celebrate pulling Vung Tau for your tour. Let's go off base and get laid!" downing his beer, making it clear he meant right then.

It was a small wooden structure, 10' x 15' with a tin roof and a blanket hung from the ceiling to separate it into two halves, him on one side, me on the other. The place smelled of incense, candle wax and fermented fish. It was dark, but I could make out one small table with a bench shoved under it to make room for the twin-sized mattress on the floor.

As I tripped out of my fatigue pants, she turned and put the MPCs (military pay currency) I gave her, about $3, into an old vase. I took advantage of the distraction and quickly slipped my wallet under the mattress.

As she removed her baggy gray shirt and baggier black pants, I could see she had a cute petite figure, but it was impossible to tell her age, somewhere between 15 and 30.

Afterwards I briefly fell asleep but woke up to a stirring next to my right ear. *This girl just might have a little passion after all.* I was on my stomach, so I turned to my right with the best look of anticipation I could muster under the circumstances, only to come nose-to-nose with a two-foot-long rat...not counting the tail.

I quickly jumped up, lifted the mattress dumping the girl on the floor, who barely missed the rat, grabbed my wallet and split. I went one way and the rat another.

I didn't know where my new *buddy* went. I never saw him again.

I walked back through the gate and asked the AP (Air Force Police) for the time. He said 0515 hours (pronounced zero five-fifteen hours). At that exact moment, we heard an explosion off to the west.

Later, after waking up from four hours sleep, I was told that terrorists drove an old French Citroën panel truck loaded with explosives up to the front of the Victoria hotel in Gia Dinh Province, a suburb of Saigon near the Chinese district known as Cholon.

First, several occupants from the Citroën opened fire on the MP on guard duty and his Vietnamese counterpart, killing both, and then they fled on foot, tossing grenades as they ran.

Across the street from the Victoria, an explosion, a claymore mine pointed at the hotel, went off. Immediately, the Citroën with the major charge blew up. That was the explosion the AP and I heard at 0515 hours.

An MP lieutenant officer of the day was making his rounds with his MP driver. They chased the fleeing terrorists, and they were also killed, probably from small arms fire or grenades.

The MP on guard duty was PFC (private first class) Patrick John Brems. He was from my academy cycle, but a different platoon. He'd only been in-country 10 days... 19 years of age.

Before I left Tan Son Nhut, I saw the Victoria. The front of the building was blown out, taking the first three floors, clear to and through the rear of the building. Only interior support walls and pillars and the two exterior side walls held up the rest of the 10-story building. I didn't know how many others were killed...didn't want to know. Counting McKenna in Georgia, that was four military police killed in five weeks. And I wasn't even at my duty station!

Chapter 5

ORIENTATION

If you were on board a Huey flying over Vung Tau in 1966, your elevation could be as low as 650 or 700 feet. That would clear the hills and ridges that ascended rapidly from the shoreline.

Today you'd have to add another 150 feet to safely clear the 105-foot statute of Jesus erected on 558-foot high Nho Mount. The Vietnam Catholic Association started construction in 1974 and completed it in 1993, three years after American tourists were allowed visas back into Vietnam.

During the fourteenth and fifteenth centuries, European trading ships frequented the area, which inspired the name Vung Tau since it means "anchorage" in Vietnamese.

The French Indochinese government named it Cape Saint-Jacques. The town sits on a peninsula, eleven miles long by six at its widest point. It thrusts out of the mainland at a west-southwest angle into the warm waters of the South China Sea.

It does not take much imagination to see its similarity to the *boot* of Italy with the toe of this *boot* pointing toward Saigon to the northwest, 60 miles as the crow flies or 90 miles (2 hours) by road. Looking down from your Huey, Vung Tau seems to sprout from the arch of the *boot* towards the mainland.

Right below this arch, near the intersection of Ba Cu and Le Loi Streets is Front Beach, crescent-shaped, running about a mile from where the ball of the foot in the boot would be to the front of the heel.

Tran Phu Street starts at the opposite end of Le Loi at the instep, following the coastline around the toe all the way to the heel and up the back of the boot almost to the mainland, changing names four times. This last stretch, for the most part, is all beach, which the MPs called Long Beach for obvious reasons.

There was also a small beach near the toe of the boot which we called Back Beach. Except for Front Beach, all of them have different names now, but those were our labels, to identify them for rapid response.

If you nosed your Huey toward the arch of the boot, ahead would be Front Beach, with VC Mountain bordering it on the left and Little Mountain on the right. Over your left shoulder and to the rear would be Long Beach. Again, these are the names we used.

The main R&R hotel is on the corner of Le Quy Don and Quang Trung streets. Quang Trung is the name of the coast road at this point.

That put the hotel one block from Hoang Dieu Street, where most of the bars were lined up shoulder-to-shoulder.

Across Quang Trung, the beach was loaded with kiosks selling booze and snack foods, mostly booze. We called them *Ba Muoi Ba* stands after a beer popular with the locals because of its cheap price. It meant *33* in Vietnamese. The label read *33 Export* and displayed the silhouette of a tiger, so it was also known as tiger beer.

Off the starboard side of your Huey, looking west and southwest, across Ganh Rai Bay, lay the vast Mekong River Delta. Jutting southwest into the sea, it's a maze of islands, rivers and swamps and the home of Khmer-era (802 to 1431 BC) pagodas, floating markets and villages surrounded by rice paddies.

The 560th's quarters were a pleasant surprise. I expected Quonset huts or tents with wooden floors (if we were lucky) at the airfield just outside of town. Instead we were billeted in a villa near the center of Vung Tau. The MPs even ate in one of the hotels.

There was a high school behind the villa. All the boys wore white shirts and black pants. Both were loose fitting and reminded me of pajamas. The girls all looked adorable in their white ao dais, the traditional Vietnamese feminine attire. The boys seemed bright and happy and the girls stunningly pretty with their long, straight, shimmering, raven hair, carrying books and chattering away like they didn't have a care in the world.

The villa itself was two one-story white, stucco buildings to the left as you entered through the chain link fence. A third building lay outside the fence, occupied by a Vietnamese family I would come to know quite well. Two other buildings were to the front and right, occupied by the 560th. There were no doors at any of the entrances.

I stayed briefly in one of the buildings to the left, just long enough to spend one or two nights and use the cold-water shower. Just long enough to experience my second rat encounter.

I was soaping up when I felt what seemed to be a warm wet mop being dragged across my bare feet. Looking down I saw a rat doing laps on the shower room floor. I thought, *that's twice, there's gonna be some rat payback.*

When my squad assignment was decided, I was put in the center building, where I would spend all but the last two weeks of my 12-month tour.

As I entered the building, to my left sat a water cooler, plugged in, but always at room temperature. There were two rooms without doors, two sets of bunks, and four lockers in each.

My bunk was on the bottom right in the second room on the left. It was an absolute necessity to use the mosquito net on each bunk. The trick was keeping a can of mosquito spray under your pillow so that you could spray the inside of the net once you dropped the sides. Even then, if any body part (elbow, heel, etc.), lay against the inside of the net while you were sleeping, that body part would be covered with welts in the morning.

Upon entering the building, to my right were two sets of bunks and a refrigerator.

Next was a large room holding what we sarcastically called our spa. It was a tiled contraption four-foot high that looked like an indoor Jacuzzi, at first glance. No such luck. It was a cistern to collect rainwater for showers.

The entire roof funneled toward a hole above this cistern. There were three feet of floor tile on two sides of it, sunken a few inches below regular floor level and slightly slanted toward a drain, making the whole setup quite luxurious by 1950's French occupation standards.

To shower, we scooped water out of the cistern (we used a #10 coffee can) and poured it over our heads several times. Soap up, repeat. Water temperature was controlled by whether it just rained, or if the water sat for several days.

At the rear of the villa, in the right corner, was a storage room. To its left, a latrine of sorts. A toilet and small sink with one working faucet which, of course, was the cold one. It was, however, a flush toilet if you poured water directly into the bowl when you finished your business. Again, the #10 coffee can.

Left of the latrine was an opening to a small square stucco room with a low ceiling and no window, with perfect acoustics for amplifying sound. This was our weapons' cleaning room for .45s and rifles. On the left side wall was a bench four-feet in height. (After 16 total weeks of basic and the MP academy training with M14s, the Army then issued us M16s.) The perfect acoustics would eventually be the catalyst for an event that would change my life forever.

The building to the right of the villa entrance was Lieutenant Latham's office, his room and the rooms of the five sergeants, four squad leaders and Master Sergeant Greene's or Top. The highest-ranking NCO in any unit was always called *Top*, short for Top Sergeant.

My second home was northwest of the villa. The provost marshal's office – police station (PMO), a one-story structure housing both us and the QCs, Army of the Republic of Vietnam (ARVN) Military Police *Quan Canh*.

Inside, a wall separated the two police units. Jeeps, from whatever shift was on duty, were always backed in to facilitate quick response. The name *Jeep* was a misnomer, the M151A1 was a Ford product called the *MUTT* (multipurpose utility tactical truck).

The most unusual item at the PMO was the Conex, a large steel reusable container about 6'x8'. It was modified with 18" square windows in the door and three sides with three lengths of rebar welded into each window. We used it as our drunk tank.

I thought our duty shifts were unique:

3 days from 0800 to 1600 hours (day shift)
3 days from 1600 to 2400 hours (swing shift)
3 days from 2400 to 0800 hours (graves shift)
then 3 days off.

The only bad thing with this system was that we never knew what day of the week it was except for the weekly dose of Primaquine (malaria medicine) given every Monday. "Oh swell! A malaria pill. It must be Monday-barf day." Primaquine occasionally caused nausea, vomiting, diarrhea and stomach cramps. Having someone puking or crapping made Mondays memorable indeed. We were thrilled to learn we would have to take Primaquine for quite a while after returning to the States.

Chapter 6

FNG

Being one of the FNGs (Freaking New Guys), I was partnered with an experienced MP. His name was Butch Pennelli. My understanding was that military police must be at least 5'9", and from what I'd seen so far, that was the case. In fact, most of us were at least 6' tall.

I don't know how he got past the height requirement, he couldn't have been over 5'6". He wore his nightstick holder upside down so that the business end wouldn't bounce against his knee. But he had the biggest *testicoli* in the squad for a little Italian. I learned a lot in the brief time I worked with Butch.

For one thing, since we were supposed to be trying to *win the hearts and minds of the Vietnamese people*, when some bar manager or owner got all bent out of shape over a minor incident like knocking over a barstool or breaking a beer glass, we would grab the customer by the back of the collar and seat of his pants, half drag, half carry him out of the bar and plop him into our Jeep. I never saw another MP faster at that maneuver then Pennelli, myself included. We would then drive around a corner and stop.

Butch would straighten the guy's shirt, pat him on the head and politely request he not return to that bar. This request, depending on the guy's attitude, was said sometimes in Butch's excellent John Wayne impersonation.

He could be quite the diplomat, not causing issues to escalate when there was a peaceful way out. He taught me that pride was a big issue with both soldiers and merchant marines, especially if they were with a girl or one of their buddies. Don't embarrass them by playing the tough guy MP unless you need to. A valuable lesson.

But if it did come to playing tough, Butch was the best. He taught me the nightstick move. If it looked like things might go south, make sure your left leg is in front of your adversary's left leg. At the first sign of a hostile move, you slam the palm of your left hand back and down on the front top end of your nightstick. Since the holder was on a swivel, that would bring your nightstick up sharply into the aforementioned *testicoli*. That usually brought things under control in a heartbeat.

At the MP academy, I was really bummed to learn that the Colt .45 pistol holsters were designed to be worn on the right side since I was left-handed. I mean, what kind of fast draw would that be? However, in Vung Tau I soon realized one used a nightstick far more often than a .45.

Before any MP was in town long, he would have a local Vietnamese craftsman make him a new nightstick with a lead slug inlayed near the tip and the hardwood two inches longer than regulation...well, except Butch.

~~~~~~

My squad leader, Sergeant Raymer, was a real piece of work. A career soldier who fought in Korea yet was still a buck sergeant. It seemed he was always getting busted, usually for defending his MPs. The rumor was that his last demotion came from cold cocking some lieutenant after climbing over the lieutenant's desk to get at him.

Our squad quickly learned Sergeant Raymer's technique for handling drunks. Another MP and I brought a Marine in for slapping around a bar girl he had spent a lot of money on but who wouldn't leave with him. We cuffed him behind his back and had him sitting on a bench at the PMO, but he kept mouthing off, cussing and kicking at us.

Sarge said, "Come up here a minute, son."

Thinking he'd found an ally, the guy jumped up and walked to the counter all smiles. As soon as he got close enough, Raymer reached over, grabbed him by his shirt front, lifted him up, and dragged him halfway across the counter until they were nose to nose and in an extremely calm, controlled voice said, "If you so much as look at one of my MPs again, I'll rip off your head and shit down your neck...you got that?" Then he shoved the guy hard enough that he fell backwards over the bench.

Originally, I thought that was a little over the top, but we all learned quickly that these guys would always try to push the envelope. When they pushed, you must push back. You'd lose all control if you let them intimidate you.

Once, while patrolling solo, I brought a guy in I had already cuffed. As soon as I sat him on the bench he started badmouthing MPs, which I ignored since we got that a lot. When badmouthing didn't prove fruitful, he started cussing at the top of his lungs. I hauled off and slapped him across the mouth. He immediately stopped, all wide eyed, mouth agape with surprise. I glanced at Sergeant Raymer...he was grinning.

My problem was I could get so angry that the adrenaline rush would make my hands shake. During a time of danger or anxiety, your body floods with adrenaline. It's pure energy and is meant to keep you safe. But my shaking hands just made me angrier because I figured they'd think I was afraid of them. Since I wasn't about to explain body chemistry to some drunken GI, it would usually end with me smacking someone, or if they were standing, hitting them behind the knees with my nightstick. That would usually force them to sit. If not, stomping on their in-step would do the trick. *My God, was my life going to be this sadistic for the rest of my 12-month tour?*

I'm sure, as with most MPs whose tours were at in-country R&R locations, like Vung Tau or China Beach near Da Nang, I felt guilty about treating another American soldier that way, whatever their offense or demeanor, drunk or sober. *"I do solemnly swear...defend the*

Constitution...obey the orders...so help me God." Most of these guys were right out of the bush, my age or younger; in May I would turn 21. They experienced all kinds of horror and death for weeks, even months at a time. They came to my town seeking what, *Rest and Recuperation?* In part, yes. But mostly they came to forget, to release the nightmare, if only for a little while. That was the paradox. These guys tried to blot out their personal terrors, soaking up way more alcohol than they could hold.

~~~~~~

The little kid ran right in front of our Jeep, waving his arms frantically, he looked scared to death and was shouting, "Dinky dau...GI, dinky dau!" ("Crazy...GI, crazy.") In my report, after talking to the bar owner, I would write: "An American in fatigues from a combat infantry unit was sitting at the bar talking to no one, even ignoring the bar girls, but consuming a considerable amount of hard liquor when he suddenly threw his glass at the wall and then started breaking chairs over the bar and upending tables, screaming incoherently."

But as Nate and I entered the place, he held a bar stool by the legs and swung it around randomly, in circles, back and forth in front of his body and then over his head. Not threatening anyone, more like he was fending off something or some things swarming over him.

As I approached, he turned toward me, still blindly swinging the stool. I ducked under, feeling the wind from it, and tackled him around the knees. We both ended up on the floor. He, flat on his back with me on top of him. I quickly sat up, straddling him, pinning his legs and then grabbed his shirt front, jerking him up into a sitting position on the floor. We were now five inches from each other's face. What I saw in his eyes was pure horror...he was not on that barroom floor, he was under the jungle canopy staring at some unimaginable nightmare.

> "War educates the senses,
> Calls into action the will,
> Perfects the physical constitution,
> Brings men into such swift and close collision
> In critical moments that man measures man."
>
> —Ralph Waldo Emerson—

Nate, having kicked the stool out of the guy's reach, circled around behind and cuffed him. We carried him out of the bar kicking and screaming.

Nate said, "You're bigger than me. You contain him, and I'll drive," or was it my suggestion? I don't remember. Either way I found myself sitting on him again, pinning his legs with one of my hands on his chest and the other on his head in the back seat of the Jeep as he tried to bite and kick, while at the same time screaming, growling, crying, and calling for his mama.

But there was another side to this coin. One night I came across a kid at 0200 hours who was on guard duty. He was sitting on a bench with his back against the building he was supposed to be guarding. His chin was on his chest, rifle across his lap...he was sound asleep. Just by his look, I could tell he was fresh out of training and new in-country. He was in direct violation of the 1st, 2nd and 11th orders of the *Orders to Sentry* (called the Eleven General Orders).

1. To take charge of this post and all government property in view.

2. To walk my post in a military manner, keeping always on the alert, and observing everything that takes place within sight or hearing.

11. To be especially watchful at night, and during the time for challenging, to challenge all persons on or near my post, and to allow no one to pass without proper authority.

Everyone was required in basic training to learn the General Orders verbatim.

I slid his M16 off his lap without waking him, and then nudged his knee with the butt of his own weapon. He stood bolt upright, terrified. I could see it in his eyes. That's when I made my decision as to how I would handle this. I stuck my hand out, palm up, crooked my fingers in a beckoning motion and said in my calmest, most controlled, best imitation of Sergeant Raymer, "Give me your ID." I slung his rifle over my shoulder as he produced the ID, hands trembling. As I wrote down his information on my notepad, he said, "I...I'm...I'm going to get into a lot of sh...a lot of trouble, huh...Sir?"

Without looking up, I sort of chuffed and smirked. "What do you think?" Then added, "Don't call me sir. Do you see any bars on my shoulders?"

Then I looked him in the eyes, slowly returned my notebook and pen to my pocket, thrust his M16 forcefully into his hands, turned and walked away.

As I rounded the corner out of his sight, I tore his information out of my notebook and tossed it. If it was an officer who caught him, he would have been up to his waist in a heap of crap. He was merely guarding a mess hall to prevent guys from pilfering late-night snacks and the building was in the center of a heavily fortified compound. But I guarantee he wasn't going to fall asleep again the rest of that night.

Chapter 7

OTHER DUTIES AND OTHER TIMES

We weren't always on patrol duty; sometimes we took our turns at static posts Main and West gates at the airfield or guard duty at our own villa.

Main Gate

After several hours with a QC and an interpreter, "shit...son-of-a ...!" I yelped, as I hopped off one of the wooden posts supporting the split rail fence surrounding the guard shack at the main gate.

I turned back toward the post to see a lizard's head protruding out of a crack in the end of it, sticking out its tongue. That's when my entire right leg from my butt to my heel went numb. I must have limped around and cursed for five minutes, much to the delight of the QC.

~~~~~~

West Gate

This gate was locked at 2400 hours (midnight), so it was only manned for day and swing shifts. It was extremely boring, except on Primaquine Mondays, because it was the furthest from a latrine.

~~~~~~

Villa Guard

We only needed to guard the Villa on graves. 2400 to 0800 hours. Whoever was on guard would sit at a card table in front of my villa billet because it had the best view of the entrance. We wore our regular MP gear plus flack vest and steel pot (helmet). We had two 20-round M16 clips stacked on the table plus the one in the rifle leaning against the exterior wall.

There was absolutely nothing to do but swat mosquitoes and be alone with your thoughts. Not wanting to over think my war and current situation, I mostly thought about the past. This, ironically, a lot of times involved war anyway.

~~~~~~

My father was born in 1894 and my mom in 1900. They met when she was 16, and they dated for a year. When the U.S. entered World War I in April 1917, my father went off to fight in France, but not before an argument with my mom. They broke up (like father, like son).

My mother married someone else, bore six children, and then her husband died. My father came home from the war, married, had four children and his wife died. So, my parents got back together. It sounds like the movie plot from *Yours, Mine and Ours* starring Lucille Ball and Henry Fonda.

No such luck. My father was rarely around. He suffered from shell shock. Since my mom was 45 and my dad 52 when I was born, I was quite the surprise. My birth didn't help dad's situation, I'm sure. He was always in and out of the VA hospital.

Since I was one of the few kids in the neighborhood without a dad, I made up a story as to why. I told my friends he was in one of the first units the Germans used mustard gas on. Years later I learned the truth from my sister Jo, he was primarily an Army ambulance driver between the trenches and the Paris hospitals. (Curiously, the same thing Ernest Hemmingway did as a volunteer before the U.S. entered the war.)

I knew the story about when my dad was just a kid on a hunting trip, he accidentally shot and killed his best friend. I'm sure that, and all the death and dying he saw during the war, caused his shell shock.

Recently I received dad's 48-star American flag that was packed away for 100 years. He carried and/or flew it somewhere on his ambulance. It's full of bullet and shrapnel holes. So, ironically, the truth turned out to be far more profound than the lie I told for years.

~~~~~~

Lieutenant, "If we stay here we're gonna be surrounded! But with our machine gunner hit, we can't make a run for it!"

Sergeant, "Sir, we've got to try."

German solider, *"Heir kommen sie her, sie kommen!"*

Thus started one of our weekly doses of what we MPs called *training films*. Rick Jason played Lieutenant Gil Hanley and Vic Morrow played Sergeant Chip Saunders in *Combat,* which was followed by an hour of *Gunsmoke* starring James Arness as Marshall Matt Dillon, combat and cops, military and police...*training films.*

The reruns were projected onto a large screen on the roof of the R&R center hotel, weather permitting. Since it was outdoors, the show always started at dusk. As if on cue, tens of thousands of bats would fly out of their caves in VC Mountain and darken the sky over our heads.

I usually sat with Bernie, an Aussie MP buddy. He spoke French, and it was fascinating to hear him translate what some French partisan on *Combat* was saying faster than Sergeant Saunders' interpreter could translate.

I would tell Bernie every week, "Not bad for a fugitive from a penal colony." Which always elicited a "screw you, Shults." Actually, it was pretty cool, especially since in basic I took an aptitude test to determine my ability to learn a new language and failed miserably.

Since it was the main hotel for the R&R soldiers, the *training films* were shown on the roof of the Rex. The place had a fancy bar with ridiculously cheap alcohol: 20¢ for mixed drinks and 10¢ for beer. During the three-hour *Happy Hour*, mixed drinks were 10¢ and beer 5¢. The idea was to lure guys away from the more expensive local bars, bar girls and prostitutes. It didn't work, even with the added incentive of not having to swallow your mixed drinks before the ice melted which would release the rat hair and feces.

There was a grand stairway descending from the roof to the ground floor. On the way down once, I heard this *plinking* sound coming from the bar. When I walked over to check it out I found Arthur Godfrey sitting on a stool, picking at his ukulele while telling dirty jokes about celebrities.

Lieutenant Latham was there and already loaded. It didn't take me long to catch up. The villa was only six blocks away but for some reason he drove into town. I ended up driving his Jeep back to the villa. It's a good thing it was only six blocks because he almost fell out twice. I ended up steering with my left hand and pushing my right hand against his chest to keep him upright in the seat. Not something you'd do often, driving for a first lieutenant.

~~~~~~

A 17-year old from my platoon at the academy had died. He was nicknamed "Alphabet" by Sergeant Byrd because he had a multi-syllabic last name no one could pronounce. We all quickly picked up on his nickname, making sure we said it in Sarge's baritone.

Word got to us, he was on a PBR (patrol boat river) someplace on the Delta in full kit (all his MP gear, plus steel helmet, flack vest, a full complement of M16 ammo, usually two 20-round clips, fragmentation grenades, and the rifle slung over his shoulder). He fell into the swampy water and wasn't seen again. He was a good-natured kid. "I don't care what y'all call me as long as it ain't late for chow." Now he was gone.

28

Chapter 8

AN UNLIKELY FRIEND

Ho Chi Minh was a friend of mine. I called him Ho Chi for short and we were definitely buds. Probably because I was always trying to hook him up with local females. It wasn't easy, since his preferences were distinctly different from mine.

One time I was riding shotgun in an MP Jeep with a female on my lap. I talked one of the locals into borrowing her for a *quickie* with Ho Chi. The poor thing was so nervous she crapped all over me and the Jeep. Fortunately, the other MP didn't mention it to anyone in second platoon, or I'd never have lived it down. "Oh right, Shults, you're the one that bitch crapped all over." I would rather be remembered for the cool things I did. I don't think getting *fragged* with incoming crap would cut it.

After all that, Ho Chi wouldn't touch her anyway. Nor would he have anything to do with any of the female monkeys I brought him.

I don't think he was gay, he was just so furiously independent, and only did what he wanted to do, when he wanted to do it. Another example of his independence was his water dish; it was an exceptionally large metal thing, big enough for him to take a bath in. But if you tried to make him, he'd fight you tooth and nail...literally. When he felt like it though, he'd get in there with his head under the water with nothing sticking out but the hair on his back and whip around the perimeter like a heat seeking missile.

He was also a pick-pocket with a clever MO. He'd start at your ankle and slowly climb up your leg, over your hip and up your arm until he could sit on your shoulder cooing and chattering all the way to disguise his intentions. Then he'd pat you on the back of the head to distract you, steal the pen out of your shirt pocket, leap to the water tower, climb to the top and laugh until he got bored, then he'd pull the pen apart and drop it.

Another time, he unhooked the dog clip on his chain, found my part of the villa, my bunk and my mosquito net and proceeded to do back flips on it like a trampoline. When I woke up, he loped back to the base of the water tower chattering all the way. When I got there, he was holding the chain to his collar and looked at me like he was surprised I got up so early. He could unclip it, but he couldn't re-clip it. Yes, Ho Chi and I were definitely *buds*.

We never figured out if his tail was cut off at some point, or if he was born without one. Maybe the reason he didn't touch any of those females was because they all possessed tails and he didn't want to date outside his species.

He was there when I arrived in March 1966, but he was killed about a month before we moved to the barracks in mid-February 1967.

When the convoy escort got back, I was the first one they told. I didn't hear it from the guys involved...it was someone else. I was told that a couple of guys thought it would be cool if the grunts on the convoy they were meeting knew the 560th MPs had a mascot. They got to the rendezvous before the convoy, so they let Ho Chi climb up a tree still on his leash, even though I had proven he wouldn't run away. The convoy came up on them so fast that they just floored it to get to their machinegun escort slot up-front. They forgot Ho Chi was still in the tree, so they dragged him several yards along Highway 1 before remembering.

I heard, when they got him back in the Jeep he spat at them a few times, as if to say, *real slick move*, and then he died.

Since this was early 1967 I guess little Ho Chi was the first Vung Tau 560th Second Platoon *MP* to be KIA. Tragically, two more young real MPs from Second Platoon would follow.

Chapter 9

MAI

Three weeks after my arrival, Butch's tour was over. As we liked to say, "It was time to hop that big silver bird back to freedom and the land of round door knobs." All the door knobs in Vung Tau, if you could find any, or find a door for that matter, were oval in the French Colonialist style.

The timing was perfect. He got his orders right before the start of the squad's last day of three days off. The six of us went out to a restaurant. We all paid for Butch. The whole squad liked him. We paid for the booze as well, and booze it up we did.

I was the last one he embraced, just before he slugged me in the arm and said something profound in his John Wayne voice. Can't remember what it was. I was really wasted. He did do one more thing that night that I will remember always, he brought me to Mai Lynne.

After the rest of the squad staggered off toward the villa, I put both of my hands on his shoulders. I wanted to tell him how much I appreciated all he taught me but decided that would be awkward but, since I had his attention, I needed to say something. "I...I bet you'll miss all these beautiful women." His eyes went out of focus for a second and he said, "I've gotta see her one more time."

Without another word, he lurched out of the restaurant. He didn't ask me to follow, but I was curious as to what kind of woman appealed to this crazy Italian and vice versa.

He headed straight for Hoang Dieu Street with all its bars, near where it ended at Quang Trung Street, across from Front Beach and the brightly lit Ba Muoi Ba stands. Being 2100 hours (9 pm), the bar district was wall-to-wall people. I was surprised he would know precisely where to find his girlfriend amid that huge crowd. But there she was.

She looked Eurasian, with the best parts of both continents. At 5'9" she was taller than most Vietnamese. Her long black hair was wavy instead of straight, and she had a thin aquiline nose. The rest was iconic Vietnamese: wide-set almond eyes, high cheekbones, and that Cupid's bow mouth, all delightful hallmarks of beautiful Vietnamese women. That night she wore a sky blue ao dai, snug at her 20" waist, all grace...and legs.

Butch spoke just a few words, his girlfriend nodded, and they headed a block up Hoang Dieu Street, turned left on a side street and then right, up an alley full of residential buildings. I followed at a discreet distance. Feeling very much the stalker, not to mention guilty, although I wasn't sure why. I mean, we went through a lot together, and I learned much from him, but he was leaving in the morning, never to return.

Something was wrong. It was their demeanor, both of them. Instead of walking side-by-side holding hands, talking, smiling, maybe tears, this tall wispy vision of sensuality was walking several paces ahead of him. Then with a jolt, it hit me. *Oh wow! Of course!* She was at that particular corner in Vung Tau at its busiest time of night, party time. She was leaning against a lamppost for Pete's sake!

The next morning was my first back since my three days off. I thought about her the entire eight-hour shift. My limited experience with prostitution, all of it in the last 10 weeks, did not fit when stood up against that image still haunting me from last night.

The Vietnamese hookers I observed in Vung Tau were far from being of interest to me. They rode on the back of scooters or in horse-drawn carriages, usually driven by their pimps. To look more American, they covered their faces with cake makeup to lighten their skin to a ghostly white, contrasted with scarlet lipstick and eyeliner surrounding their eyes, slightly altered to try and reshape those naturally beautiful almond eyes, eye shadow in sparkly silver or gold or even green. Tight sequined dresses so short that if they bent over at the waist, you could almost see their shoulder blades. Finally, their teased hair was usually bleached blond *ala* Sandra Dee. They batted their false eyelashes at anyone drawn to the sight of these strange apparitions.

The woman last night looked more like the high school girls near the villa rather than any hooker I'd ever seen, except she was perhaps 10 years older and 3"-5" taller. Maybe she wasn't a prostitute. Maybe I just read the situation incorrectly. I was very drunk. But I knew I was kidding myself. Not that it mattered anymore. At this point she could have been Lizzie Borden. I wanted to be with this woman.

All through brushing my teeth, re-baptizing myself with the #10 can at the cistern (more than enough times), putting on clean fatigues, and combing my hair, I was wondering what she would say if I gave her extra money, so I could spend the night, or if she even did that, or if any prostitute ever did that. That's how little I knew about them.

Of course, she didn't have a door, but instead there were several rows of beads, enough to block any view of the interior. Once inside, to the left was a full-sized bed draped with an oversized OD mosquito net, straight ahead was a table with bowls, cups, chopsticks and the inevitable candles and incense. To the right, surprisingly, was another room with chairs, lamps and a small round table holding a transistor radio and a 9" black and white TV. Between the rooms was a small bathroom with a sink and a flush toilet with an actual handle to do the flushing.

She was living better than we were. It was then I decided to ask if I could spend the night if I gave her more money. She smiled, wider than I would have expected, and took the $5 from my left hand and proffered $3 in her right.

On the bed, now, I produced my trusty prophylactic. She cupped my hand in both of hers, gently folded my fingers into a fist. "No, I take care." Now that could be interpreted in at least three ways, but I was completely in a "whatever you say" mode by then and tossed it aside.

In the morning I dressed and started for the door. As I parted the beads, I felt a tentative finger tap on my left shoulder. *Wow, she wants to give me a goodbye kiss, how cool is that?* Making myself believe I must have really impressed her, I slowly turned, all suave-like, and my mouth fell open in total bewilderment, surprise and delight. She was standing there with the $8 in her right hand.

"I give back, you come see me more."

I nodded numbly with my mouth still open. She laughed at my silly expression, put two fingers under my chin, closed my mouth and then kissed me.

I got halfway back to Hoang Dieu Street when I realized I still didn't know her name. I returned to ask her and...I spent another hour. Thus, began the most unusual relationship I ever had with the opposite sex up until then. It remained the most unusual relationship for the next 12 years until just before the start of a Denver Broncos football game at 2:00 p.m. on October 1, 1978 in Glendale, Colorado.

Chapter 10

IN BLACK & WHITE AND COLOR

As three of us walked into our villa after one of our day shifts, we found that the other three from our squad had set up a movie screen and projector. The black and white image looked like Back Beach close to sunrise. The projectionist said "You gotta see this. Graves filmed it two weeks ago."

As the camera panned the small beach, something came into view. Indistinct at first but slowly washing further onto the beach with every wave of the incoming tide. Not rolling, just twisting at the feet as the waves did their work. *Feet, bare feet,* now the arms moving in the surf like a horrifying attempt at a *snow angel.*

Someone barked a laugh, thinking it was some idiot messing around, and then quickly stifled it as reality sank in. "Who...who is that?" he asked. "Just some Gook," the projectionist said.

"Just some Gook." His loose black pajamas were above his knees and his loose white shirt above his emaciated torso. One eye was swollen shut, the other, the iris turned white, stared unseeing at the sky. But it was the mouth that captured the attention. It was perfectly round, a shape that could not happen in life, *the size and color of a tarnished silver dollar with a large hole in the center.* Slowly, we all began to titter weakly, because that's what you did if you were a *tough guy* MP. I was thinking of those high school boys I saw on my first day...I laughed nonetheless.

That short black and white film turned out to be just a preview. The full color version followed just two days later at the end of my second day of graves. Some FNG who took Butch's place and I *(now I was the trainer...too soon),* were called to Long Beach to check out another body.

This one was face down, features buried in the sand. Still intact but much more decomposed than the *black and white* body. His clothing and stature indicated he wasn't American. Therefore, not our problem. But a crowd of locals was gathering, and I wanted to show concern.

I asked the new guy to turn him over. He slowly but emphatically shook his head no, not taking his eyes off the corpse. The body's right arm extended out from his side. For some reason I didn't want to dwell on, there was a short piece of planking attached to his wrist with rope. I bent down, and without looking, groped behind me with my right hand, hoping to grab the piece of plank and praying that the rope still attached plank to wrist. I missed and grabbed his forearm, somewhere midway between his wrist and elbow. Soft, like surgical tubing full of pudding.

Wanting to get it over with, I stopped feeling for wood and stood up with whatever it was I held in my grip, intending to step over him, lifting the arm with me to pull him over on his back. What I didn't intend was for all flesh, muscle and sinew to detach from his clavicle to his elbow and slither down over my hand. I also did not plan on the smell that was released, along with several bloated sand crabs that quickly scurried away, *again the tarnished silver dollar.*

The gag reflex is powerful, as well as painful when you try to suppress it. Cheeks full of bile, I squatted in the surf, swallowed and washed my hands, trying to do it slowly and deliberately as if I simply had gutted a fish I'd just caught and wanted to rinse off.

It was after days like this when Mai Lynne was my greatest comfort. We would sit cross-legged on her bed as I tried to explain, in extremely poor Vietnamese, what I saw and did.

Although I doubt she understood much of it, she always picked up enough to show empathy. Then she'd frame my face in her hands, lean in close enough to touch noses, and rattle off several sentences in French, in a voice sounding more like teasing than concern. Then she'd laugh at my bewildered expression. That made me laugh; which, I suppose, was the whole point. I guess I could have asked Bernie by trying to remember and repeat her French back to him phonetically, but Mai Lynne had a way of making me forget.

Walking along Quang Trung Street one afternoon, both of us watching Sampans moored offshore at Front Beach, their sculls swishing back and forth disturbing the glassy surface, Mai Lynne did a double take toward one of the Ba Muoi Ba stands. Then pointing, she said, "He not pay yesterday." Stopping, I asked, "Which one?" She paused a second, as if regretting what she said, "that one," pointing again, this time with less enthusiasm. I walked over to the guy, Mai Lynne in tow.

"Hey, shit head."

He turned on his stool looking first at me then at her, then back to me. By then my hand was out palm up, beckoning with my fingers. The same gesture I used on the sleeping guard at the mess hall. No Sgt. Raymer voice, no words at all. He pulled the $5 worth of MPC out of his shirt pocket and aimed it toward me, proving he recognized her and knew her prices. Still not saying a word, I nodded to my left toward Mai Lynne. He shifted the money to his right hand and offered it to her. Mai Lynne looked at me as if she needed my permission to take it. I said nothing, so she did, hesitantly. As we walked off, her arm linked in mine and her head on my shoulder, I was feeling gallant and chivalrous. Then it hit me, I guess I was now officially her pimp.

I only hesitated for half a step. As if divining my thoughts, she stopped me with her free arm, turned to face me, and placing her hand gently on my chest she looked up into my eyes, "I sleep no more MP." Then, "Just you, always." Her tone of voice told me it wasn't a thank you

35

for what just happened, it was a fact since that first night, and it didn't have anything to do with money, now or in the future.

From that point on I saw our relationship as the plot from *Irma La Douce*. With Mai Lynne in the title role as the soft-hearted hooker instead of Shirley MacLaine and me as Jack Lemmon's Nester Patou, the French police officer.

There was a small sheltered cove just before the beach road changed its name for the fourth time and bent toward the northeast clear water, white sand, one narrow path down, cliffs on three sides framing vermillion sunsets and pink-edged clouds. The tiny beach gave birth to riptides, making wading above the knees precarious.

We would simply lie on the beach, soft sand as our blanket, surf caressing our legs and make out. Burt Lancaster and Debora Kerr in *From Here to Eternity*.

Chapter 11

MUSIC TO MY EARS

Like Butch, Jack Garchow was one of my heroes, mainly because he possessed the *testicoli* to extend for another year. He was assigned to Tan Son Nhut, Vin Long and finally Vung Tau. He had a great voice and played an acoustic guitar. He usually sang country and western songs. He even wrote some. I first met him during my short stay in Tan Son Nhut where he was visiting MP buddies. He put new words to an old Marty Robbins' song:

> "To a far and distant country,
> came a unit one fine day.
> 'Twas the 560th MPs,
> they were there for quite a stay."

The MP brass (officers) and their minions thought it was the best patriotic song since Barry Sadler released *The Ballad of the Green Berets* three months earlier. Every time an MP officer spotted him, they'd ask him to play it. He was usually embarrassed, since he only wrote the words and not the music.

When I first ran into him in Vung Tau, he was busy writing the lyrics and music to another song about the unit. He also wrote humorous little ditties, one about a Vietnamese girl who liked an American soldier who was so young he still had acne issues. A line in the chorus, *"Oh pizza face, I rub you so."*

Another one of his groupies and I would sit around, hanging onto every word of every song. He owned a tape recorder, so we would breathe a high-pitched exhale that on tape sounded exactly like thousands of cheering fans. It was more fun than *training films* on the R&R center roof with the bats.

Jack was definitely a singer-songwriter, but he couldn't draw at all. Having only 75 days left on his second tour when we met, he started his own FIGMO chart (military acronym for *freak it, got my orders*), which we used to express disinterest in our current assignment or job, given that it would end soon. The chart was always a drawing of a shapely lady. Mostly outline except for three particular parts of the female anatomy, plus facial features.

When you reached 100 days left in-country, you started shading in the 100 little sections the figure was divided into. The 3, 2 and 1 were always the same three particular parts.

Jack saw some of my drawings lying on my bunk and decided it would be infinitely better if I drew him a new chart. This made sense as his looked like an amoeba with the trots. When I finished, he enthusiastically filled in the first 25 sections and duct taped it to his locker.

Having only 100 days left was a much bigger deal than just posting your FIGMO chart for all to see. You were a *short-timer* and called yourself *short*. That morphed into endless exclamations as to just how short you were.

"I'm so short I can sit on the edge of a dime and dangle my feet."

"I'm so short I'm gonna start sleeping on a lower bunk."

"I'm so short you can't find me under my own helmet liner."

"I'm so short I can hide behind my nightstick...even a legal one."

Sometimes it would get so annoying, we wished they'd just leave.

When it came time for Jack to leave, it was the same routine as with Butch, dinner in town and booze. Fortunately for Jack, he had an early flight to Ton Son Knut, so we walked him back to his bunk to get some sack time.

Not the rest of us. Oh no, that became known as the night of the *Great White Toilet Paper Incident*, or *TPI* for short. We went to an unoccupied part of the villa. Someone produced both a bottle of Scotch and a bottle of Tequila – I don't remember who – possibly me? Then we sat cross-legged in a circle, four or five of us. I don't remember that either. The plan was to pass around the Tequila, swigging right out of the bottle, and then chase it with the Scotch. Someone dubbed this the *MP Drink*. I don't remember who – possibly me. After much gagging and choking with booze coming out of noses or running down our chins, I lost track of the action. Conveniently, there was an exit at the back of the building, no door, of course. Less conveniently, there was an open sewer back there I wasn't aware of. In the morning, whoever woke me up discovered my foot was in the open sewer with toilet paper wrapped around my ankle. I'd rather have confessed to the monkey crap incident than endure the razzing I got for that little stunt.

Chapter 12

CALLOUSNESS AND CONSOLING

I was on solo patrol driving along the coastal highway adjacent to Long Beach. There was a crowd of 15-20 clustered 10 yards from the water's edge. Vietnamese girls were hugging each other and crying or standing alone, hands over their mouths, bodies trembling.

I pulled off the road, getting as close as I could before hopping out. Wading through the crowd I found a bikini-clad Vietnamese girl, 13 or 14, lying on her back, *school girls by the villa?* There were two Americans in civilian clothes, doctors or medics, trying to revive her. I assumed the Americans came from the R&R-operated Beachcomber bar across the highway.

Two civilian cops were just standing there, arms folded, doing nothing. So I attempted crowd control. "Stand back, these guys need some room, give them some room." To the girls, *"Dừ ng lại, dừ ng lại,* she...she'll be okay."

Twenty minutes after I arrived, she was not okay. She was dead. Both guys looked at each other, then stood up. Louder sobs, more girls hugging. No other sounds save the screeching of a seagull. Since she wasn't American, there was nothing more I could do. So, I moved away, as did most of the crowd. I heard my Jeep radio squawk, so I sped up, passing two soldiers in fatigues. I heard one say, "I would have *boned* her while she was still twitching." Then both laughed.

I reflexively stopped and turned around. They looked at me as if to say, *What? You got a problem?* I saw their patches and knew that their unit was just out of the deep bush, and they saw a lot of hard fighting. They pulled R&R at the same time and were drinking at the Beachcomber. I turned and walked to my Jeep.

During my brief time in-country, I had already realized one can experience just so much death and dying before becoming desensitized. Sitting at the R&R Center bar or any local bar, it didn't matter, we heard stories that would make your skin crawl: NCOs making necklaces out of guitar wire and human ears, guys jamming a four-foot length of rebar into each of a corpse's ears and propping it up on the two gate posts of their compound. My own unit circulated a photo of a grinning ARVN Ranger holding two decapitated heads by the hair.

The day of the drowning I walked to Mai Lynne's after my shift ended. I knocked on the exterior wall next to the beads. Several minutes later, she poked her head out. Pulling the beads back together at her chin, she formed her mouth into an apologetic pout and shook her head. This wasn't the first time that happened and wouldn't be the last. I walked back to the villa, sat on my bunk and waited. Thirty or forty minutes later, someone would shout, "Shults, your girlfriend's here ... again." She came to the villa on her Vespa and had it turned around. She'd be looking over her shoulder, wearing one of her fanciest ao dai and cracking that amazing smile.

Later, we'd hop back on her Vespa and head for Long Beach and the Beachcomber or one of the Ba Muoi Ba stands on the ocean side. Or we would walk to Front Beach then turn northwest. She developed an aversion to sitting with me at any of the stands on Front Beach since the confrontation with one of her johns. Unlike with Butch, she would walk by my side holding my hand. Or walk her favorite way, arm hooked in mine, head on my shoulder. It was much slower, but speed wasn't the point. I think we both needed the physical contact. It helped each of us let go of our personal demons.

Also, that part of the boot toward the toe put us geographically the furthest from the more distasteful activities of my day...and hers. The landscape slowly rose up from the ocean so that eventually you would be above the many flat-bottomed sampans anchored off-shore with colorful paper lanterns hanging from thatched-roofs, flames dancing on the off-shore breezes. Across the street, small homes, lighted windows, and the smell of meals being prepared, rice and shrimp or pork but always the pungent odor of *nuoc mam* (fish sauce).

Since Mai Lynne owned a Vespa scooter, she saw no reason to ride in the most used and over-used vehicle in Vung Tau or in all South Vietnam. I was always talking her into riding with me because they were so unusual. They were simply weird – weird and funny.

The Lambro 200 or the 550. The 200 possessed one headlight, the 550 two. The 200 was named after its engine size, 200 cubic centimeters. The 550 after the amount of weight it could carry. Lambro was a division of Lambretta, a three-wheel version of the two-wheeled Lambretta.

The driver sat just behind the single front wheel in an enclosed box-like structure with no door. Looming behind him was a large, open-sided rectangle with no back wall centered over the two rear wheels with two benches along the sides facing each other.

Since American GIs were a foot taller and twice the weight of Vietnamese, a Lambro could carry eight of them or four of us, if you didn't mind bumping knees.

The only American-made cars were all early 1950s because they weren't imported after the French were defeated.

Chapter 13

Mayhem and Marriage

Bob Bailie, a close friend since grade school, somehow managed to talk a couple girls into sending me letters. Having no girlfriend at home, this was the next best thing. There was also mail from Bob, a few other friends and, of course, family. Consequently, I had my *mail call* pretty much covered.

Then, much to my surprise, I received a letter from someone I least expected, my ex-girlfriend. She was pregnant. In my world, in the 1960s…at least in upstate New York, if you got a girl pregnant, you married her.

I got her letter in early May, three weeks before my birthday. It would take two months for Battalion to grant a 30-day compassionate leave. During those two months I rode my first convoy escort and used my top-secret security clearance for the first time.

The day before the convoy, a guy from the 72nd Airborne parked his Jeep in the PMO compound. Obviously, he was straight out of Indian Country. His vehicle was caked in dried mud, windshield hinged down and covered with sand bags to protect the occupants from ricochets or shards of glass. To prevent cables strung across a jungle road from decapitating both driver and passenger, there was a four-foot high wedge-shaped protrusion thrust up from the center of the front bumper, like a middle finger extending from a clenched fist, and a M60 machine gun mounted between the front seats, 7.62 cal. brass casings littering the floor. What caught my attention was his M16 hanging outside behind the driver's door like a Winchester rifle slung on a saddle in a western movie. *This I absolutely had to do for my first convoy!*

It was certainly a cool way to flaunt 560th MP escorts. I spent a lot of my downtime scrounging up spare web belts and a piece of burlap to rig my rifle just so. Unlike with my .45 caliber pistol, I could use my left hand. I arranged the top of the stock, so it tilted forward in the burlap so when I reached behind me, I could grab the handle that was mounted at the rifle's center of gravity just above the pistol grip, trigger housing and ammo clip port. Then I practiced my quick draw several times to make sure I had it down pat.

Just as we were about to leave the villa to rendezvous with the convoy, I got a last-minute passenger … Lieutenant Latham! I knew I would have someone riding shotgun (literally), but I didn't figure on the lieutenant. Especially with my weapon rigged like John Wayne in *She Wore a Yellow Ribbon*.

I put up the Jeep's canvas roof because I felt a few drops. By the time we reached the convoy, it was pouring. That's the way it was in

Vietnam, either it wasn't raining, or it was pouring. By the time we got all the convoy vehicles rolling, the dirt roads were a quagmire.

A convoy lineup was usually MP Jeeps in the front, in the middle and in the rear. The front and rear would have the .50 caliber machine guns and all three would be in radio contact. Thirty miles out my radio crackled, then squawked, "*Dừ`ng lại! dừ`ng lại!*" "Stop! Stop!" We just sat there for half an hour. I never did find out why. You'd think as the MP escorts, they'd tell us.

I was getting antsy and must have had a brain freeze or something because I forgot who was riding shotgun and thought I'd try my quick draw again. When I whipped my weapon out of the burlap, being wet, it slipped out of my hand. When I lunged for it, I only succeeded in knocking it further away and deeper into the mud. The guy manning the M50, who was standing up and saw the whole thing, thought it was hilarious. Lieutenant Latham, not so much. For a second I thought about bringing up the last time I drove for him … *maybe not.*

Between the convoy debacle and the first use of my top-secret security clearance, Sergeant Raymer was transferred out of the unit. The story I heard was that some drunk balked at being thrown into the Conex and grabbed the rebar in the front window and wouldn't let go, so Sarge broke a couple of his fingers with a nightstick. Much to my surprise, he wrote me once from his new unit but didn't mention getting busted or the $5 he owed me.

Our new squad leader, Sergeant Cooper, was a nice guy, but us MPs that arrived in Vung Tau at the same time and in the same squad ended up getting *short sheeted* on promotions because of the switch in sergeants. It was time for our reviews advancing us to SP4s from PFCs (specialists 4th class from private first class), and all our squad leader needed to do was approve it.

Most sergeants simply okayed the promotions when they crossed their desk. However, Sergeant Cooper denied them, claiming he wasn't familiar enough with our skill sets. The result was that several MPs with less time in-country and indeed, in the Army, were higher ranked than we were. More importantly, it meant less money since it affected both our rank and hazardous duty pay.

A week before I received the orders for my compassionate leave, I was required to deliver a locked satchel (I didn't have the key), to the 18th Military Police Battalion headquarters in Saigon, something only an MP with top-secret security clearance did. I wore full kit: fatigues, steel pot, flack vest, M16 with two 20-round clips duct taped together for quick flip insertion (should I find it necessary to empty the first one), plus all my standard MP gear of nightstick, cuffs, .45 with 7-round clip inserted, and two extra clips on my belt. *Just like Alphabet before he drowned.*

My hop to Saigon was on board a de Havilland DHC-4 Caribou, a dual prop aircraft with a large drop bay door under the tail that became a ramp for loading cargo. That's how we boarded, by walking up the ramp and sitting in canvas sling seats facing the center, myself and two guys with engineer corps insignia. Someone from the cockpit said, "You're gonna want to strap in guys."

He wasn't kidding; before they completely raised the cargo bay door, we took off at the usual extreme ascent. The three of us are now at a 45° angle staring down at a rapidly shrinking runway and then the Mekong River Delta, all three of us holding a fist full of canvas seat strapping until we leveled off and the ramp closed. The landing was uneventful other than the usual extremely steep descent.

On the ride to the city by military shuttle, my attention was drawn to a large compound surrounded by a heavy gauge wire fence and topped with concertina wire (coiled razor wire). It was full of Vietnamese. Some looked dejected, others defiant. Most of them in loose-fitting black pajamas, some in various uniform parts, OD like ours, all of them barefoot. One of the MPs guarding them looked familiar.

Headquarters seemed to be in the middle of the city. Traffic was unbelievable with pedestrians; bicycles; scooters; Lambros; fifties vintage cars; trucks of all sizes, civilian and military; Vietnamese cops standing in the middle of intersections not doing any good at all. They held whistles between their teeth, which they may or may not have been using because a cacophony of bicycle bells, vehicle horns, old mufflers, and the shrill whine of over-loaded Lambros drowned them out.

After delivering my satchel to a lieutenant colonel, the one with the key, he told me to stay put while he checked the contents. Then he looked at my name strip as if to confirm something. Grinning, he said, "If you want to call home, the phone bank is at the USO across the street," adding "Your mother contacted battalion through the Red Cross, worried because you haven't written her for a while." I didn't know if the grin was for safely receiving his top-secret security dispatches or because he figured he was dealing with some *mama's boy*. Fearing the latter, I quickly saluted, about-faced and left.

The phone bank sounded like a great idea. I could talk to both my fiancé and my mom. Unfortunately, the lines were so long we could only make one call. Mom was the one that contacted battalion, and I certainly didn't want some NCO back in Vung Tau reminding me to *call your mommy*. There was also the fact that I hadn't spoken to my soon-to-be bride since the argument that ended with our breakup just before heading for Vietnam. I wouldn't have known what to say. I needed that 10,000-mile, 18-hour flight.

My emotions were all over the place. I was trying to be the best MP I could, there were friends that depended on me and me on them. I was still learning, still had a lot more to learn, and now I would be leaving for a month. Then, of course, there was Mai. How was I supposed to change gears so quickly?

I called mom.

"Hello, mom. Uh, over."

"Bob? Hi, honey."

"Mom, you're supposed to say 'over'. Umm, over."

"Over...we all miss you."

"No, you need to say 'over' when you're finished saying something, over."

"What? Err, over."

"The overseas operator needs to know when you're done so she can switch--"

"We're done so soon? Over."

"No, mom, we're fine. So, what do you think of being a grandmother again soon? Over."

"Yes." Then, "Is it safe where you are?"

"Sure, but it's safer at home with..." then,

"Mom, I've got to go, there's, there's a line behind me. Over."

That didn't go well. A harbinger of things to come?

Passing the prisoner compound on my way out of town, I spotted the same MP. This time it hit me; it was Jim Samples who obviously had survived his bout with spinal meningitis. He most likely recycled to the class behind us at the academy. Frantically I tried to drop my window on the shuttle, but it was stuck.

~~~~~~

The night before my hop to Saigon and home, I spent with Mai. I didn't know how to tell her, so I told her nothing. If she sensed something was on my mind, she didn't show it. We were up late, walking. First to the northwest and the sampans, then back by Front Beach and continuing southeast toward our little beach. *I must be out of my mind.* There was a pretty little gal in the States that I would be seeing in less than 30 hours and marrying her within the month, yet I was torn about not seeing this person again, this prostitute of all things! *This whole thing really stinks. I hate this, I hate everything.*

"You want to go beach?"

"No."

Armed with my month's supply of Primaquine, I boarded my flight out of Saigon. The whole 10,000 miles and 18 hours I didn't think about what I was going to say to a pregnant fiancé I hadn't seen in three months when our last conversation had been an argument.

My thoughts were full of, *what shift would I be on right now? Would the FNGs know to check the alley behind Hoang Dieu Street for curfew violators sneaking out of the Rex? Who would help Bernie with drunken Aussies? Did I tell Sergeant Kim I was leaving? Could you really suspend a dead body between gate posts using rebar? Why did drowning victim's mouths look like that? Did that drowned 13-year-old go to the school by the villa? Was his wrist still attached to that piece of plank? Did anyone know about the dangerous riptides at the little beach besides me and Mai Lynne? Mai Lynne ...*

Bob Bailie drove my fiancé to the bus stop. They were both standing there as I stepped off. She didn't look four months along, which was amazing since she was so petite. *Almost a foot shorter than...* I must have been a surprise as well, having gone from 210 to 179 pounds in that same four months.

The first person we went to (I wasn't even sure what to call them. Father, pastor, minister, reverend, sir?) asked us a lot of questions. We lied, never mentioning the baby or anything we thought he wouldn't approve of. He eventually asked us if we were believers. *Believers of what?* That's when I told him about the little Bible in my helmet liner.

"So, you carry a Bible around for good luck?"

"Umm ..."

Eventually, he said he didn't feel it would be right for him to marry us.

The next one we lied to as well and threw being *believers* into the mix. He said he would perform the ceremony. Bob was my best man.

Chapter 14

Many Happy Returns

Twenty-five days after I stepped off that bus, I was stepping onto a four-prop military Super Constellation headed for Travis Airbase near San Francisco. I figured out my leave down to the day. I planned to spend two days and one night at my sister Jo's place (she was now living in Berkeley) and then head back to Vietnam out of San Francisco. *The greatest plans of mice and men often go awry.* Twenty-seven months later I would feel the ramifications of this plan gone awry.

Engine trouble forced a landing in Fort Wayne, Indiana. We would be spending the night at the air base. Thinking myself clever, I followed protocol and contacted Sergeant Greene, telling him the situation and saying I would be a day late, knowing that would prevent them from writing me up as AWOL (absent without official leave).

Also, that way my plans could still include Jo without getting in trouble. Most of us slept in the TDY (temporary duty) barracks. Some went to town. One guy claimed he'd picked up a stripper at a bar and spent the night at her place. We heard about it all the way to Travis.

Jo, her husband, Pat, and I had a terrific time. We went to a bar that billed itself as a place Jack London had frequented. I was amazed it wasn't condemned as a fire trap. In fact, there was a fire at one time. They simply left the charred beams and pillars in place and re-hung photos of Mr. London. We ate some place on Fisherman's Wharf, where my wonderful big sister became quite angry because I couldn't prove I was 21, (the legal drinking age in California at the time). "What! Oh, so he can go to war for this country, but he can't drink?" When they dropped me off at San Francisco International, Jo, with tear filled eyes said, "Honey, if I ever have a son, I'm going to name him Bobby."

As memorable as that was, a visit to Presidio Army military fort on the tip of the San Francisco Peninsula was the most notable because it struck me as the perfect posting to top my *dream sheet*. If you served in a war zone, you got to pick your next duty station. You'd list three or four because you wouldn't necessarily get your first choice.

Landing at Tokyo Haneda International, I needed a cab to get to Tachikawa Airbase. As a taxi screeched to a stop at the curb, two hands reached for the door handle, mine and that of an Army chaplain.

"Sorry, sir. You take it."

"Where are you going, son?"

"Tachikawa, sir."

"So, am I. Would you like to split the fare?"

"Sure, sir. Uhh, yes sir." I was still a little intimidated by mid-rank officers. Especially men of God, perhaps since I recently lied to a couple of them.

"I pray this driver knows ..." He cut off his sentence when he bumped into me as the cabby lurched away from the curb. "Oh my," were his next words as our backs slammed against the rear seat. I was grateful to be riding with a chaplain. Every time I glanced to my left, he was crossing himself.

Tokyo traffic was as bad as Saigon's, only newer and faster. The other difference was that most pedestrians dressed like Americans. Mini-skirts were in vogue. I don't know what the chaplain thought, but I wasn't complaining. I briefly got a look at a large rooftop billboard showing a tiny, boxy car, and thought that would never sell in the land of the Cadillac Eldorado and Lincoln Town car. Even the name was a hoot and certainly appropriate. I drew out each syllable, emphasizing the first one, *TOY-o-ta.*

My third air hop was Tachikawa to Tan Son Nhut on board a Lockheed C-130, possibly the most uncomfortable aircraft I've ever been in, a four-engine turboprop military cargo transport. It felt like the inside of a *Shake and Bake* bag with me being the chicken leg for 2,700 miles.

That was appropriate since across the aisle from my canvas sling seat were several cages of live chickens, also a couple of rusted bicycles and a goat. If you needed to pee, you walked to the tail which pitched up at that point so one leg was higher than the other while you peed into a funnel. The goat peed where he stood.

My new squad leader picked me up in one of our unit Jeeps. As soon as we shook hands, he reached into his fatigue shirt pocket and handed me a Primaquine tablet, I'd forgotten it was Monday.

As we headed for the villa he told me that the massive American troop build-ups and the number of refugees fleeing the north were rapidly increasing our workload.

With that, he said he needed me on graves that night, so I'd be going back on duty at 2400 hours (midnight). It was now 2330 hours. Thirty minutes to shit, shower and shave for guard mount. Just like old times at Fort Dix.

At 0020 hours (12:20 a.m.) I walked the alley off Hoang Dieu Street looking for GIs sneaking out of the Rex. Maybe it was the smells: salt sea air wafting in off Front Beach, candle wax, incense, damp canvas, *nuoc mam;* or the sounds: laughter from the open hotel bar windows, whispers from Vietnamese kids who should have been on their mats asleep, or the sounds of the waves on the incoming tide; but it suddenly struck me that I had really missed all of this.

I thought about the plans I'd made at guard mount. Since this was the last night of graves, I was going to meet the other MPs at the Beachcomber around 1500 hours. This was nothing new. We usually met someplace at the end of every set of three graves and the start of our three days off. *I really did miss this.* We stuck together off duty, usually at a military run R&R facility because, like cops everywhere, others don't want you around unless they need you. The only other choice for sanctuary was with your Vietnamese girlfriend.

It was then that I caught movement off to my left. Someone slipped into the narrow space between the third and fourth buildings east of the Rex, obviously trying to hide from me. These kinds of things happened often, but this was my first in a month, and what did Sergeant Cooper say about an influx of refugees? Could some of them be VC? Expecting some drunken American or Aussie but preparing for the worst, I tested the pivot on my nightstick holder with my left hand, thinking *GI,* and unsnapped my .45 cal. holster with my right, thinking *Charlie.*

By the time I reached the space between the buildings, he was halfway to Hoang Dieu Street. That's when I caught a glimpse of yellow. It was the stripes of an American Army staff sergeant, Three up-one down. I let out the breath I didn't realize I'd been holding.

"Military police. Nice try, slick. Now turn and face me."

As he turned he said, "What time is curfew?"

I was about to say it started 20 minutes ago when I recognized that deep baritone voice. Sergeant Byrd looked, not at my face but at my name strip. He appeared to recognize the unusual spelling.

He said, "One of ma pidgins done come home to roost on me."

Of course, I didn't write him up. I just escorted him back to the Rex.

"Did you ever hear from that girl again?"

I said nothing. Long story, short walk. I watched him weave toward the side door of the hotel and then disappear behind it. *Take care, Sarge.*

Since graves ended at 0800 hours, I was in my bunk at 1000 hours and up by 1500, five hours sleep not being much after all that traveling and a full eight-hour shift. But that's when I'd agreed to meet the others at the Beachcomber. I wanted to get back into the mix.

Four of us squeezed into a Lambro for the 1½ mile ride, knocking knees the whole trip.

The 'comber' was a low, flat-roofed building, eggshell-colored stucco with flowers painted on the outside. Much bigger inside than you would expect. It had a large bar, run by Americans, and a stage that was occupied by a Vietnamese band with the female singer in a clinging miniskirt.

As we walked in, the two other guys from our squad caught our attention by waving a half-empty pitcher of beer. The girl and her male counterpart were attempting the Nino Tempo & April Stevens' version of *Deep Purple.*

Right off the bat, "So Shultsy, you knock up your girlfriend before you left knowing that you'd get 30 days out of this shit-hole of a country?"

"At least the one I knocked up had round eyes," I said, nodding toward the MP across from me. He said nothing. I was back in the mix.

The male singer crooned Dean Martin's *Everybody Loves Somebody.*

I never drank beer at an R&R bar for the logical reason that I could get drunk twice as fast on Scotch and soda for only 5¢ or 10¢ more per drink. But, since beer was the drink *du jour,* and in pitchers no less, I decided to go with the flow, so to speak.

Nate Shanker was in my platoon at the academy, so I told him my Sergeant Byrd story. This led immediately to all of us singing military police marching songs at the top of our lungs. First the clean ones, then the raunchier ones from basic training with Nate and me leading in our best Sergeant Byrd baritones. This did not please the band, but we were MPs, so we didn't care.

After several hours of drinking beer, something I wasn't used to, the band started playing *Itsy Bitsy Teenie Weenie Yellow Polkadot Bikini.* I stood up and headed for the door. By the time I got there, I forgot why.

Then somebody reminded me. "Didn't that Vietnamese chick drown right across the street?" For some reason I needed to find the spot. Unsuccessful, we ended up stamping on sand crabs. I heard someone say, "I wonder how long it would take to swim home."

I woke up without my fatigues, shrouded entirely in an unfamiliar silky material. All around me were white clouds floating on warm breezes, then a light beyond the clouds and a silhouette. It was seeing the naked angel that affirmed the fact that I was dead. She had long wavy raven hair, was 5'9" with a 20" waist, all grace and legs. Then the clouds shifted, the silk parted, and we were two together, warm and safe in the clouds.

As we sat cross-legged on her bed, noses almost touching, Mai told me I showed up soaking wet to the waist, my face moist with tears. She illustrated this with two fingers tracing down my cheek, and then framing my face in her hands she said in French, *"Mon depute fou."* She laughed at my confusion. I didn't. Then she pointed out her new silk sheets and told me she replaced her old double sized OD mosquito net with a new opaque white one. Then I laughed, and she looked confused.

We spent the next day visiting our old haunts, including a ride to our beach. We could have walked, but Mai Lynne knew my affinity for Lambros. It's possible we would have knocked knees with her at 5'9" and me at 6'2" but, of course, we sat side by side. At the beach I thought about how she never mentioned my protracted absence and even suggested the Lambro to please me. In fact, the entire day seemed to be a long *I forgive you*. I could only assume she felt her own profession allowed for some missteps on my part.

Chapter 15

Okay, addressing the obvious, how did I feel about my other life, relative to this thing with Mai? I felt nothing. I didn't even think about it.

I can only explain it as having no moral compass at all. None of us seemed to. The military did absolutely nothing to discourage promiscuity or even adultery.

Whether it was a film or speech on protection from venereal disease, or an admonition to be sure and register the whore you're bringing up to your hotel room on R&R in Singapore so she doesn't rob you blind, no one ever said "All right, all you single guys listen up," or "Okay, married men, plug your ears." On the contrary, I've heard the prophylactic speeches open with something like "All you married guys especially, listen up, because we don't want you bringing home a surprise, whether it scratches or squawks, to the little missus."

An even cruder way I've heard it expressed was "Hey, I'm putting it out there for my country, why can't I have someone *put out* for me?"

"Gee, Bob, aren't you glad we didn't let you swim back to the States? You wouldn't have been able to spend the night with your other blushing bride." That was my greeting when I slid off Mai Lynne's Vespa at the villa entrance, said half in jest and half in justification of their own *missteps*, past, present and future.

~~~~~~

Main Gate

Four hours into a slow day shift I needed to pee, so I headed for the back of the guard shack. Quang, one of the QCs, also had the same idea. I saw a couple of paper cups lying on the trash-littered ground. So, for no particular reason, other than mind-numbing boredom, I decided to push one of them around with urine. I happened to glance to my right to see Quang just turning toward me at the same time, realizing we were both abusing paper cups in the same way. For some reason this struck us as extremely funny. Still laughing as we returned to our posts, the little female interpreter didn't know what we thought was so funny and we weren't about to tell her.

~~~~~~

Villa Guard

My mother's brother, Les (where my brother got his name) was in World War I. He died of the Spanish Flu in 1918.

My brother George was in World War II. He never told our sisters about what he went through. Sister Jo said he and dad would sit alone on the porch and talk in hushed tones about their respective war experiences. George died after a short illness at 56.

My oldest brother Ernie was also in World War II. After seeing that his young son was with friends, he used his deer rifle to take his wife's life and then his own. I don't remember a lot about it, and since I was only 10, I wasn't told much, but I got the impression from siblings that it was *related to the war*. By now they were calling it combat fatigue.

~~~~~~

My favorite duty, whatever the shift, was International Patrol. That's when I was able to work with Bernie and Sergeant Kim, plus a QC and sometimes a white mouse. The civilian cop, of course, being irrelevant. About the time Bernie parked the Land Rover and got to the bar followed by the QC, Kim was cuffing the still-prone and groggy ROK (Republic of Korea) Marine, and I realized the inside of my left thigh was bleeding.

"Who's the drongo?" Bernie asked, noticing who was standing over the Marine.

"Who gives a shit, I'm bleeding."

"See that little pouch on your belt, mate? You got an Ace bandage. How 'bout you just use it?"

"Yeah and you can kiss *mon cul.*" Having two sources, my French was improving.

Sergeant Kim was still grinning, something he did a lot when he wasn't *kicking butt and taking names.*

We left our Marine with a Korean foot patrol and piled back into the Aussie Land Rover. Since it had a larger capacity than our vehicles, it was more practical for International Patrol. Kim usually rode shotgun. I liked to stand up in the back holding the roll bar with the QC. It was a better vantage point, looked more intimidating and it didn't hurt that it made me look taller, since any given QC was usually less than 5'5".

The idea was for each of us to handle our own countrymen, coming to each other's aid only when necessary. The Aussies were the biggest problem, so I was always helping Bernie. But in civvies, it was hard to tell the Aussies from the Americans, until they opened their mouths.

Bernie: "Show me some ID."

"Screw you mate!" That was your first clue. Australian men hated authority figures. Americans, most of them, were more docile when caught doing anything they knew they were not supposed to be doing.

Eventually Bernie and I worked out a system where one of us would ask for an ID as the other eased around behind the suspect. If the guy mouthed off (in either *Aussie speak* or *real English*), whichever one of us was in the back would pin the guy's arms to his body while the other cuffed him. Bernie simply bear hugged him until I slipped on the cuffs. That was also my method until I was *mule kicked* in the *testicoli*.

After much trial and error, I learned to slip my arms under the armpits, then lock my fingers behind the neck and jump up on the guy's back. If his knees didn't immediately buckle, my weight would eventually bring him down...eventually. The first time it worked, even Sergeant Kim was impressed, sort of.

"I tell you what, Bob, you gotta be slowest American in Vietnam."

One of Sergeant Kim's men was going home, so he threw the guy a party. I was invited. It was all MPs and all Korean, except the Vietnamese kid bartending and making sure that the plastic bowls were full of pretzels and chips, very stale, most likely left over from the last party.

Knowing Kim as well as I did, I held a lot of respect for Korean MPs. And all Koreans seemed respectful, unless duty required otherwise, or they knew you well enough to wisecrack.

I'm not sure if it was out of respect for me or tradition, but they did not talk amongst themselves, which would leave me out (most spoke extremely poor English). Their tradition might have been singing. That's what we did for three hours, waving our drinks around like party favors. Some of the songs must have been patriotic because they would stand up and sing even louder, something I didn't think was possible. When I thought I recognized a tune, I would try to sing the American words. When I didn't, it was just an unbelievably bad job of lip syncing.

As the evening wound down, Sergeant Kim got everyone's attention and said, in a solemn voice that sounded rehearsed, "Okay, now we sing good American song for my friend, Specialist Four Crass Bob Schra"...[fade away, he never could pronounce my last name].

> *"You are my sometime, my only sometime.*
> *You make me happy when skies are green.*
> *You'll never know, dear, how much I rub you*
> *Please don't take my sometime away."*

Then they all stood one more time and solemnly sang *Aegukga*, the South Korean National Anthem. I didn't even try to attempt that one. I was still biting my lip in an unsuccessful effort not to laugh over *my sometime* and *how much I rubbed her*.

Kim drove me home in his Jeep. I managed to not fall out, even with no help from the driver. When we pulled up to the villa, we were still singing about our respective *sometimes* and *green skies*.

Chapter 16

FAMILY TIES

"Đến đây MP, Đến đây, GI chiến đấu!" Some Vietnamese words I quickly picked up. "Come here, MP, come here. GI fighting!" I followed the kid to the bar and found two naval officers, a commander and a lieutenant commander, the former standing feet apart, right foot ahead of the left, hands raised and folded into fists. The latter sitting on the floor, hands behind his butt for balance, not looking like he wanted to get up.

This was my first hostile encounter with officers, mid-grade no less. It was constantly drummed into us at the academy that we held authority over officers when it came to police matters if we followed proper protocol. I never quite got that, so I was winging it.

Addressing the commander, "Military police, what's going on, Sir?" I made sure to spit out the last word like a sour grape. That seemed to work. Taken aback, he slowly lowered his now-open hands with quick, nervous glances to either side.

Behind me I sensed the lieutenant commander slowly getting up but increasing his distance. I was spaced equally between them. They were three feet on either side of me, I took a couple of steps back so both could see my expression and body language.

I spread my arms in exaggerated perplexity as in *well*? Or, *are you stupid?* Both started speaking at once. Then both stopped. Then the lieutenant commander started again, more or less, "I...I...I'm...he doesn't...I don't have any...."

This was getting nowhere so I turned to the commander. The commander, pointing, said "this son-of-a-bitch was screw...bothering my wife" and followed with a list of ports of call in which he searched for this guy, finally running into him in a bar in my town.

Fearing this was rapidly turning into a scene from *Casablanca*, I said, "I don't care, Sirs!" Another grape.

"You're both officers, not longshoremen!" *Too much?* Nothing from either, so I guessed I was still on a roll.

"Now, gentlemen," I spat "I suggest you split up right now and one of you follows me."

The lieutenant commander actually raised his hand. Outside, I asked him if he wanted to write up a report. He said "yes," so I drove him to the PMO where he changed his mind, saying he was leaving in the morning and just wanted to forget about it.

We were standing in front of the MP desk by then, so Sergeant Cooper asked me to drive him to his hotel and asked if he felt he needed an escort to his ship in the morning. He said "no."

That morning was the switch from swings to graves and I planned to sleep in. At 0500 hours, "Shults, wake up. Some Navy dick wants an escort to his ship. He specifically asked for you."

~~~~~~

Little Anh and her brother were the first of our villa neighbors I met shortly after I arrived in March. I was thinking about the water cooler, the one that I already realized was always plugged in but never cooled anything and being the wise guy I always strived to be, I asked, "So where's the coke machine?" bending over to pet Ho Chi as if addressing him.

"It's right there, smart ass" one of the sergeants said, pointing toward our neighbors.

"What?"

"Yeah, the family next door sells us cold Cokes all the time."

Since we were standing next to our ammo Conex, which backed up to the wire fence separating us from our neighbors, little Anh must have picked up on the word Coke, probably the only English word she knew. She couldn't have been more than 2½ years old, and the smallest person I'd ever seen who was that mobile.

"Coke? Coke?" Enormous dark eyes, bangs to her eyebrows, hair to just below her Cupid's bow mouth and a smile from ear-to-ear. She came teetering over to the fence, flip-flops threatening to desert at every step, with her brother close on her heels. He was supposed to be the Coke broker for the MPs, but not if little Anh could help it.

Her brother said, "You new MP?" stepping in front of his sister. "Me, Thang."

"Your name is 'Me Thang'?"

"No. Thang. My sister, Anh."

"How old is your sister?"

He held up three fingers but said *hai*, which meant two, something I'd learned from watching ARVN drilling "*Một hai ba bôn*," (one, two, three, four). Closely watching her brother and thinking that "more is better," Anh held up all 10 of her fingers, looking triumphantly at him then back at me and smiling.

"How old are you Thang?"

"Bay" (seven), holding up the correct number of fingers and grinning, revealing a missing baby tooth.

The three of us became instant friends. Actually, the four of us: me, Thang, Anh and Ho Chi, the monkey. Little Anh would always come to the fence when I wanted a Coke, holding onto the back of Thang's shirt and tripping over her flip-flops, then asking for Ho Chi, who I would bring to the fence for the three of us to pet.

I would not know the names of the rest of the family until August, but it was a grandfather, grandmother, a daughter (or daughter-in-law) and her husband and their two kids. The woman was about four months pregnant.

The husband was gone during the day, so Thang handled the Coke sales – Thang and Anh. Since they stored the Coke inside their part of the villa, we never knew how they kept them cold and we didn't particularly want to know, thinking of the rat hairs and feces at the local ice plant. I guess it didn't matter since the Cokes were in bottles.

Interestingly, they knew Mai Lynne and greeted her with, "Xin cha`o, Mai Lynne" whenever Mai dropped me off or picked me up on her Vespa and Mai would wave.

Chapter 17

A "WIN-WIN" SITUATION

It was now late August, Mai dropped me off at the villa around 0200. Day shift guard mount was in six hours.

As soon as the sound of the Vespa died in the distance, I heard scuffling noises coming from Thang and Anh's place. Their mother had the new baby now, and it could be her nursing, but it sounded agitated and frantic.

I don't know where the rest of the family was, but the baby lay in his little crib crying, and his mother was cowering in the shadows. It was dark except for a perimeter security light from our side of the villa. She was backed into a corner, her hands flat against the two walls.

A shape lurched out of the shadows between the two of us, civilian clothes, about my height, too tall for a Vietnamese. He must have seen her looking over his shoulder because he staggered a half step sideways and turned toward me. All I could see was a crooked grin...a beckoning grin, as in, *join the fun.*

Now she was sliding toward the baby, keeping her back against the wall. I shook my head and the grin vanished. He took three steps toward her and I shoved him against the wall at the spot she just vacated. His face was out of the shadows now, the face of an MP.

Then the grin again as he shoved off the wall and came at me. There wasn't much of a tussle. I shoved him again, this time with my left shoulder. Against the wall again he slid down and landed on his butt. Getting up on his own, he left.

When I got off at four that afternoon and passed by our neighbor's yard on foot, frantic arm movements from grandma caught my attention. She was standing in the middle of their property. Her right side toward me, hunched over, head bobbing, smiling, with betelnut-stained teeth. Not taking her eyes off me, she began sidestepping back toward her place, repeatedly slapping her thigh, like she was calling her favorite pet. Beyond her, most of the family was waving me forward, Anh, using both hands.

As I walked under the arch into the same room I left less than 14 hours earlier, Anh took one of my arms and Thang the other, escorting me to a 6'x8' bamboo mat in the center of the floor, grandma close behind.

The grandfather, and his son or son-in-law, were squatting, as only Vietnamese can on tiny 5"x5"x6" high stools. It was still light out but there was a candle at each corner of the mat. Soon the grandmother settled in as well.

Now only the children's mother remained standing near the crib, naked to the waist, her back turned chastely toward me as she finished nursing the baby.

Most Vietnamese mothers wouldn't do that. They nursed, whenever, wherever, however they pleased. She then placed the baby in his crib, buttoned up and went into another room.

Knowing 6'2" frames didn't fit on 6" high stools, they borrowed a chair from the MPs. Realizing that was just as impractical, since the mat was on the floor, I sat cross-legged at the mat, which pleased the elders, now two betelnut-stained sets of teeth.

"Đến đây mẹ" from the other room and the grandmother disappeared as well. When they returned, their arms were laden with steaming bowls of rice, shrimp, pork and some kind of mystery meat and, of course, Cokes.

It seemed the mystery meat was the appetizer since everyone ate it first. It looked like rawhide shoelaces on steroids and was as tough as rawhide and salty...and delicious. Much Pidgin English and sign language later, it turned out to be dried squid. It was hilarious watching everyone half cupping their hands and wriggling their fingers like squid tentacles.

After watching a lot of head bobbing, both nodding and shaking, along with much finger pointing, I finally learned that Thang and Anh's mother was the grandparent's daughter. So, the father was the in-law, who happened to work at the ice plant, which explained the consistently cold Cokes. Little brother's name was "Dat."

Both surnames were Nguyen, which is not surprising. Nguyen was the family name of a major Vietnamese royal dynasty. Many members of the Ly family from the prior dynasty changed their name to Nguyen to avoid persecution. Americans would pronounce Nguyen, Nguyen as "Win, Win." *A win win situation for me.*

About an hour later, I returned the MP chair to its proper location, escorted by two little Vietnamese kids.

More head shaking, this time from bewildered MPs. This meal ritual went on for the next six months at the beginning of every other swing shift cycle...every 24 days. I wouldn't find out how they kept track of my work shift cycle for another seven months.

A few times I tried to explain to the Nguyens that I knew that MP and I was sure he would have given up on his own, but they would hear none of it. Besides, how do you explain something like that in Pidgin English and sign language?

I'm sure Thang and Anh didn't know why I was the family MP VIP, but they jumped right on board. In addition to the Coke and monkey ritual, they always waved when they saw me coming or going from the compound, occasionally not wanting to take my money for the Cokes. But I always paid. Partly because the money could go toward my dried squid.

No MP, including myself, was exempt from the family wrath if they caught you abusing a glass Coke bottle. You were supposed to return the bottles in pristine condition, as they were reusable.

And heaven forbid if you broke one. Little Anh would stomp over to the fence, not even worrying about an abandoned flip flop. She'd stand there, feet apart, little hands fisted on her hips and, through scowling lips, let out with, "Ho Chi mad!" One could only hope she meant the monkey, not the Prime Minister of North Vietnam.

Chapter 18

A "BLOODY" MESS

It was graveyard shift, almost 0200 hours. I was driving east on Hoang Dieu, checking bar windows for backlit silhouettes over 5'5". Locals were more than willing to accommodate GIs violating curfew, their money was still good, whatever the time of day. In fact, they would facilitate this by switching to candlelight after midnight. But, there were other ways to spot GI silhouettes besides height, most Americans slouch and all of them had short military haircuts.

In a good mood and humming *Silhouettes* by the Rays, impulsively I turned left onto Thu Khoa Huan Street and a quick right up Mai's alley to see if any lights were on behind her beads. Hoping they weren't, because it would mean she was alone, since nobody would want to be around Mai Lynne and not be able to see her.

Her lights were out, but 50 feet further up the alley I heard several young Vietnamese voices, menacing, threatening, *Cowboys*. Choosing to remain in the Jeep, because that's where the radio was, I drove slowly, since the alley was narrow and full of bikes and a few scooters, including Mai's Vespa. Thirty feet closer, I saw four or five shadows dart across the alley headed back toward Hoang Dieu, spooked by the sound of my approaching Jeep.

As I figured, they were *Cowboys*, our euphemism for local juvenile delinquents–teenaged boys with nothing better to do than hassle drunks of all nationalities. They didn't care one way or the other about the war, except that more people simply meant more victims.

Their MO was intimidation, both in numbers and a guttural combination of Pidgin English and Vietnamese. They often faked martial art skills, air jabs and foot swipes, ending with "gimme money!" This was one of the reasons we were so hard core on curfew enforcement.

Before turning right to follow, I glanced left. A GI was leaning against the side alley wall in a sitting position, his left arm limp at his side. His palm was up and filling with blood.

Forgetting the *Cowboys*, I went to him. His eyes were open and staring, he was shaking, and going into shock. Of all things, my Boy Scout first aid came back to me. I gently laid him prone and slid a small wooden crate under his heels to elevate his feet.

His left forearm was bleeding profusely, laid open from the inside of his elbow to his wrist, *a machete*. Holding an Ace bandage between both hands I spun it into a single strip of gauze. I wrapped it around his upper arm near his armpit, hoping to close off the main artery.

Now I needed something narrow about 6" long to complete my tourniquet. Finding nothing else, I tied in one of my .45 cal. pistol clips. I twisted it until the blood stopped pulsing.

The guy was coming around, so I asked him if he could hold the tourniquet taut while I helped him to the Jeep and drove him to the doctor or medics at the airbase.

He nodded, so we were off, red lights on either side of the windshield flashing, siren blaring. An Army doctor was on duty, a captain. He said something about the tourniquet as he handed back my .45 clip caked in blood.

Then, after swabbing the wound, and giving him a couple of shots of pain killer, the doctor started stitching the guy up. At around two dozen stitches I stopped counting. Since the guy was stationed in Vung Tau, I called his unit and his sergeant picked him up.

The next time I saw Mai, I told her about the *Cowboys* and the machete incident. Mainly because I liked how she responded to my stories of trial and tribulation, but I didn't tell her it happened in her alley.

~~~~~~

"MP, MP, GI quan canh." The bar I was led to this time was smaller than most, made even smaller by the wall just inside the door, not of brick and mortar but of flesh and bone. The guy must have been 6'5", 250. He had me by 3" and 70 pounds.

His back was to me, civilian work boots, jeans, and a leather vest revealing an 18th century sailing ship tattoo on the back of his left arm and part of a large anchor tattoo curling around from his right bicep. *Grizzled old merchant marines who carry every hand weapon known to man.*

When first approaching a confrontation, we were trained not to touch anyone until we identified ourselves as military policemen. That struck me, this time, as a really swell idea.

As I tested the pivot on the holder of my extra-long, leaded nightstick, although I doubted it would bail me out this time, I stepped far to his right, far enough to be out of reach if things went south.

That's when I saw his adversary, if you could call him that, 5'7", dark-rimmed glasses, loose fitting Air Force uniform–the only thing missing was a pocket protector. Seeing no threat there, I turned back to the big guy.

"Military police, what's the problem?"

Big guy: "I'm gonna deck this little sum' bitch."

Little sum' bitch: "For some reason he wishes to engage me in a round of fisticuffs."

Me: "What?"

Little sum' bitch: "For some reason..."

Me: "Yeah, I heard you, and if you keep talking like that, I'll deck you myself."

This made the big guy laugh so I figured he was on my side, at least for the moment. Before he could think too much about it (although I didn't feel thinking was his strong suit), I said, "Why don't you and I just walk out of here?" I made sure it sounded like a suggestion, not an order.

Much to my surprise and extreme relief, he nodded. And we just walked out the arched doorway, not at the same time, I doubt if we'd both have fit.

At the sidewalk, we went east on Hoang Dieu. Twenty paces later I looked over my shoulder and little sum' bitch was coming out of the bar and headed east as well...until he looked up and saw us, did an about-face and headed for Front Beach.

~~~~~~

Villa Guard

I have only four memories of my dad. The first was when I was about three, possibly my first memory ever. I needed a pen to draw with, but Les was doing homework, using the only one we could find, so I was told to wait. Not liking to wait for anything, when he was *finally* done I dropped it down the heating vent. (I guess being the youngest and the only child from mom's first love, I was spoiled.) My father put me over his knee and spanked me. I remember mom picking me up and holding me until I stopped crying...like I said, I was a little spoiled.

On my tenth birthday, grandma brought me to the VA to see dad. We sat on a screened-in second floor porch, because dad said he needed some fresh air.

Before heading to the VA, gram made the mistake of telling me she bought a BB gun and would give it to me later at her house.

The disabled vets fascinated me out on the lawn with missing arms and legs, or walking with long white canes, tapping them on the ground or swishing them back and forth. I couldn't understand why dad was there when he didn't seem to have anything missing.

Whenever I could tear myself away from the disabled vets, I would ask gram about my present. Dad got upset because I was more interested in other vets and my BB gun than I was in him.

In 1965 when I was 20, Jo flew out from Utah and she and I went to see him. He was close to death. He thought I was his oldest son, George.

A week later was the fourth and last time. He was in his coffin. Dad's side of the family seemed surprised that I was there.

Chapter 19

I'm not sure the first organized show we saw in Vung Tau was part of the USO. It didn't seem to be their style.

There were three sets of temporary bleachers forming a U-shape erected behind the Rex. None of us off-duty MPs knew what the show was, only that it was free. We left our happy hour drinks at the bar to check it out.

We were in the shade because the sun was setting. The first to appear onstage was a strange-looking guy with a Hawaiian shirt, shorts, and flip flops, long hair on the sides and back but balding on the top. He was holding a microphone and calling himself "Mr. 5x5," which is exactly what he was, five feet tall and five feet wide. He sweated despite the shade. He was the MC introducing three strippers, all slightly overweight, slightly over-the-hill and more than slightly sweating.

What followed was the raunchiest strip show this side of The Blue Fox in Tijuana. We heard they got word of it all the way up the ladder to MACV (Military Assistance Command Vietnam). The result was no more strip shows of that type in R&R centers, ever again. I imagine they thought the GIs just out of the bush were already traumatized.

The only legitimate USO show to reach Vung Tau during my tour was Nancy Sinatra. To me the only thing topping that would have been Ann Margaret or Joey Heatherton. I realized, much to my horror, that I was on duty that night. Fortunately, as it turned out, my duty was to be security for Miss Sinatra.

Jimmy Wicks and I were to sit front and center, first row, 15 feet from the stage, in full MP regalia. *These Boots Are Made For Walking,* being her biggest hit, she wore high-heeled boots almost to her knees, and a miniskirt (as short as those worn by most of the Vung Tau hookers). She pranced around the front edge of the stage for the entire performance. Jimmy and I were required to sit there for 2½ hours. A dirty job, but someone had to do it.

After the show she was driven in a military staff vehicle to her hotel. We followed in our Jeep. Two of her band members were in our back seat. As a truck came toward us, it's headlights revealed the driver of the staff car plus Nancy and some officer in the right corner of the back seat, both seemingly occupying the same space.

I said, "Please tell me they aren't swapping spit!" It was more of a statement than a question.

First band member, laughing: "That's exactly what they're doing."

Jimmy, "What's the story up there?"

Second band member, "It's the same story up there and everywhere," chuckling at his own play on words. "She does that with every logistics officer in every location we have a gig."

Quite a patriot...that Nancy.

~~~~~~

Walking several blocks east from Front Beach on Ba Cu, it ends at the intersection of two major streets, Le Hong Phong and Truong Cong Dinh. We considered this the center of town and only a block and a half from our villa and the high school. Locals ran shops on all five corners.

Most of the bars were on or near the beaches. This left room for everything else, laundries, tailors, restaurants, a movie house, photo developing and tattoo parlors. All shops tried to cater to the GIs.

The sidewalk near every corner was crowded with pushcarts selling one kind of snack food or another. All of them sold pho, a Vietnamese concoction made with beef or chicken broth, scallions, cilantro, onions and thin slices of meat. Also, most of them sold my new favorite appetizer, dried squid.

One of the shops was a candy store stocked with every conceivable kind of candy I never heard of. After much trial and error, I discovered one that reminded me of circus peanuts, at least it was that same flavor with a different consistency, shaped like ladyfinger cookies and they came three in a pack. I realize now that they were, more or less, Turkish Delight (jellies covered in powdered sugar), in only one flavor.

Two or three times a week when I was off during the day, I would walk the block and a half from the villa and buy four three packs, one for me, one for Thang and little Anh and two I'd divide between the six kids that always followed me there.

It was always the same six kids. One would attach himself to me near the high school and the others one at a time all along the way to the candy store, chanting *"keo, keo, keo."* I felt like the Pied Piper. They weren't begging, they were just bouncing along behind me, singing; so how could I resist those six pairs of big brown eyes?

Occasionally one might not be there, but I never figured out why it was always the same kids. Or why they only followed me when I was in civilian clothes, not in my MP uniform.

~~~~~~

Six exhausted MPs walked into our billet shortly after 2400 hours, at the end of swings. It was a busy shift for everyone. It started with two Chinook helicopters colliding at the airbase. Next an AWOL apprehension. Two officers arguing about who ran over some dog. Stolen fish. A couple fender benders. A broken shop window. Not one, but two, hookers crying rape because, as was usually proved to be the case, their Johns didn't pay for their services. The inevitable barroom confrontations. And ending with a guy who was so drunk, he passed out face first in his pillow and died of suffocation.

We were all so wired we knew we wouldn't be able to sleep. This had happened before, so we didn't even try. All one can do is wait for the adrenaline to dissipate. Four of us in the one room, just lay there on our backs, hands clasped behind our heads, staring at a leopard gecko feeding off insects flitting around our single, bare light bulb as we talked about the shift.

Once we covered all the day's events, we got to talking about things that happened on other days and other shifts:

Nate Shanker, southern boy, who loved peanuts in his Cokes and imitating Sgt. Byrd, "Shultsy, remember the overturned Jeep and the big red smear?"

"How could I forget?"

"Yeah, we were way out on Tran Phu when up ahead we see this overturned Jeep, its wheels still spinning, and this reddish-purple smear..."

"Bloody smear," I added.

Nate continued, "It ended with this glob of what looked like ground beef with these bone white pieces of something mixed in. Bob called in this traffic fatality way the hell out on Tran Phu, because of this brain and skull smear. Just as we stopped behind the Jeep, this guy comes out of the woods..."

I added, "With this stupid grin on his face, waving his one hand at us and trying to button his fly with the other. He was totally shit-faced."

Nate, looking down from his upper bunk and across the room at me: "Turns out it was ground beef and the white stuff was waxed paper."

"What are you looking at me for? You thought it was brains too!"

"Yeah, but you were the one that needed to explain the radio call."

Jerry said, "Shultsy, you and Pennelli were tight. Did he tell you about the tattoo parlor credit scam?" Jerry Napier was the guy I nodded toward across the table at the Beachcomber when somebody brought up the subject of knocked-up girlfriends. Jerry's locker is full of photos of his wife and lately, a newly opened box of Trojan prophylactics.

"No, never heard that one."

"This local tattoo artist shows up at the PMO with three signed IOUs for tattoo work he'd done. These guys claimed they'd square up with him out of their next month's pay, but they never showed up. The names they signed were obviously bogus, and the local didn't have a clue, but he did know their unit from their patches. So Butch and I take the tattoo guy to the airbase."

"As you know, Pennelli would be the first to say we must 'win the hearts and minds of the Vietnamese' and to never disrespect the concerns of a local, but he just couldn't play this one straight. He made the whole unit turn out in formation. Butch stood there, all 5'6" of him, feet apart, and nightstick in his left hand smacking it against his right palm and he said in his best John Wayne impersonation, 'Alright Pilgrims, Donald Duck, Batman and the Lone Ranger...front and center.'"

"Yeah, kind of like the MPC thing," this from Jimmy Wicks. "You know how MPC looks like fake money anyway? Well some signal corps' guy got his parents to send him all the paper money from his Monopoly board game. Then he and his buddies started spending it all over the center of town. They told the merchants it was the latest issue MPC."

Shanker told the ground beef story, so I just lay there watching the gecko finish off the last of his late-night snack. Then said, "I wonder if it's the same lizard in here every night?"

Nate, "We could brand him," Then added, "y'all."

"I think there's paint in the room next to the shitter," Jerry replied.

Four guys hopped off their bunks at two in the morning and headed for the storage room. We found a half-empty gallon of white paint and the four-inch brush the motor pool used to stencil Jeep bumpers.

The ceiling was high, so Wicks climbed up on his bunk, dripping paint brush in hand. But the light bulb was in the middle of the room, and he couldn't stretch that far. So, I leaned against his bunk and he got on my shoulders. I took a few steps forward and he swiped at the gecko and nailed him on the first try.

The gecko is now covered with white paint from just behind his eyeballs to the end of his tail. The problem is that the gecko was a half inch wide and the paintbrush was four inches wide. The ceiling was beige, so now it also had a white swatch next to the light bulb...until the lizard moved, and there was a beige swatch on a white swatch on a beige ceiling.

When we finished laughing, Jimmy said, "We need a BB gun."

Someone, "What, you gonna shoot the gecko?"

"No, no. I'm just tired of trying to run over rats on graveyard shift and missing. We could shoot'em with the BB gun."

The villa guard called from the porch, "If you guys don't shut the hell up, I'm going to shoot all of you."

Chapter 20

QUAN CANH VS. CANH SAT

I'm sure you've gotten the impression by now that the military police thought little of the *canh sat* (civilian cops). The QCs were cool because they were tough little guys. But the white mice (civilian cops) weren't called mice just because their uniforms were white. Any time there was any action, they'd either just stand there and do nothing or slink out-of-sight.

An example of both slinking out of sight and doing nothing was the time I got stuck with a *mouse* on motor patrol. At the heel of the boot where Ha Long turns to Thuy Van Street, near Mai's little beach, there is a small natural plateau with steps leading up to it carved out of the rock. On the other side is a path down to a cove with two docks the Navy used to ferry sailors to and from shore leave. They would gather on the plateau to wait.

As we rounded the bend, I saw about 30 guys on the plateau, arguing and shoving each other around. They were most likely from at least two different ships. I pulled the Jeep over and started up the rock stairs. I looked behind me, and the white mouse was slinking down below the dashboard of the Jeep, out of sight. I was about to face 30 drunken sailors alone.

"Military police, this stops now!"

I hear someone say "We ain't Army pukes."

And another, "Its only one guy."

Quick glance behind me, back down the rock steps and all I can see is the top of a white hat.

Now I hear, "Come on, it's only one freaking MP." Surprised, because I never encountered Navy guys that aggressive before, something kicked in from the academy, *it's usually mob mentality or just courage in numbers, and Sergeant Byrd saying "just bluff 'em,"* so I started shouting at the top of my lungs.

"Shut your mouth, shithead" and "You, too, asshole!"

And to a third, "The next time you open your mouth I'm gonna shove his head up your ass!"

As I said this, my left hand was on the butt of my nightstick and my right on the now unsnapped flap of my holster. I kept up my tirade with every obscenity and threat I ever heard in all my time in basic and MP academy combined.

Nobody was more surprised than I when they all shut up, got in line, and headed, in silence, down the path to the docks. I figured they thought that if any guy was crazy enough to stand up to 30 drunken sailors, he'd use that .45. After I got back in the Jeep, I sat there a while until my hands stopped shaking, enough to shift the Jeep into reverse.

I wanted to tell the white mouse to get out of my Jeep and walk back to town. But I didn't. *Hearts and minds.*

Chapter 21

REST AND RECUPERATION

It was now early September and I was due for my three days out-of-country R&R. There were a couple of opportunities to head out for the three days but the empty seats on the planes were empty because someone was killed or wounded, and taking their seats just wasn't something I felt I could handle.

Wicks was also due for his R&R and Singapore was the first destination offered. It sounded good to both of us. After a 700-mile flight, we landed at Paya Lebar airport where a civilian bus and an Army officer were waiting.

The officer, a lieutenant, gave us the speech about registering any *lady* we might want to bring up to our room (so she wouldn't rob us blind, since she would have to leave her local government permit as a disease-free legal prostitute with the desk clerk), and he added that cabbies were the best source for getting a hold of them. Then he announced, much to our delight, that the USO arranged for a pool party at our hotel with several college girls from a local English-speaking campus.

The girls were sweet and all empathetic about our Vietnam duty. They wore modest one-piece swimsuits and never came closer than three feet from any of us. For every girl there were three chaperones.

As soon as the party was over and after all that splashing around in the pool with a bunch of college girls, Wicks and I promptly called a cabbie.

The hooker's place was a nice-looking four-story building only about eight blocks from our hotel. The cab driver said "second floor" and gave us an apartment number, saying he'd wait and take the four of us back to our hotel.

Two women between 30 and 35, wearing robes, greeted us at their door. One of them, quite pretty, long curly brown hair, 5'6", Asian, took me by the hand and led me to a closet and asked me what I wanted her to wear. Thinking about the cab ride through Tokyo with the chaplain, I pointed to a miniskirt and blouse.

In the morning, after they collected their permits at the front desk and we saw them to a cab, we boarded a waiting Mercedes bus for a prearranged tour of Singapore.

The bus driver must have been in cahoots with every merchandise peddler in the city. Every time we stopped at a traffic light, which was every block, he would open the door, and a different guy would get on and walk down the aisle handing out flyers and directions to his shop.

Just before the light turned green, the rear door would open, and that guy would get out.

After the tour, for some reason, we decided to go bowling. The Chinese man on the next alley wanted to talk. Eventually we realized it was yet another guy trying to lure us to his shop, this one by driving us in his car. He tried the promise of booze, drugs, and prostitutes, to no avail. All three were readily available in Vung Tau. So, we were unimpressed.

Then he said he could give us the phone number of two British Army nurses ... his car was big enough for all of us to sit on the bench seat up-front. Of all things, there was a 45-rpm record player hanging under his dashboard and wired to his power source. He deftly switched records and out of his scratchy, popping speakers came Elvis Presley's *G.I. Blues*.

His shop was small but, you name it, he sold it: chess sets, dolls, ceramics, glass jewelry, charm bracelets, sunglasses, watches, hash pipes, everything. But first things first, Jimmy asked for the phone number and I called it right from the guy's shop. (You'd have to get up early in the morning to con this MP.)

Much to my surprise, a young female voice with a British accent answered. I told her we were two American GIs on Rest and Recuperation from our tour in Vietnam (pointedly using the words, not the initials) and we'd like to get together. She said they'd be delighted to meet us and gave me the address. We each quickly bought something cheap and hailed a cab, still not sure that this was for real. Two classy ladies in uniform met us at the door, not women in robes.

It was a great time for all and we were perfect gentlemen. We went to a restaurant of their choosing, Chinese naturally, danced...that was something of a challenge, try dancing to the only song on the Jukebox I recognized...the Beatles' *Yellow Submarine*.

The high point of the evening was after dinner lingering over our drinks (Singapore Slings, of course), these two proper British Army nurses looked at each other and nodded, as if agreeing it was the right time to ask.

They both leaned forward over the table and in a somber tone, one of them said, "You two must have experienced some pretty...intense things over there, do you mind telling us about them?"

Then the other added, taking Wicks' hand and patting it gently, "We mean only if you want to talk about it." We both leaned in close as well, and in equally somber tones I said, "I saw Nancy Sinatra necking with an Army lieutenant," and Wicks added, "I painted a lizard."

Chapter 22

MIND GAMES AND MEMORIES

I headed to the PMO for guard mount and the start of swing shift. Alone in my Jeep I thought about how much the influx of refugees was changing the face of Vung Tau.

Now there were shacks everywhere. If you could even call them that. Tiny pathetic structures cobbled together with 4x8 sheets of uncut aluminum beer cans, corrugated metal and even cardboard. Rare were the thatched roofs since the Nipa palm trees used to make them were stripped bare by earlier refugees.

Naked little kids played in filthy puddles. Small dogs stood alone, hind legs twitching from the onset of rabies. Grandmothers squatted over open fires, just barely off the road, preparing whatever they could scrounge up to eat.

On the other side of the peninsula lay the city dump. I'd watched an emaciated old man in worn sandals, short pants and torn print shirt squat over a pile of what might have been gravy, egg shells and rancid meat. Having grabbed a damp sagging cardboard box, he scooped his little pile into it. Every other handful went to his mouth, blowing on them first, to shoo away the black flies.

I jolted back to the present as I rounded a bend and saw a five-ton truck that had hit a horse cart. The horse was dead, the cart driver was dead and a little girl around nine was sitting by the side of the road, feet in the ditch, crying, blood from a cut on her forehead mixing with her tears.

It was a civilian truck. The accident had nothing to do with Americans. So, again, it was not my problem.

I went to the little girl first. She was now trembling as well as crying, more of a deep agonizing wail. I tied one of my two Ace bandages around her forehead, but she brushed it off with the back of her hand. She started shaking, shock again. I applied the second bandage. As she reached up to brush it off as well I said "*dư`ng lại*, honey *dư`ng lại* you need to keep this..." then it was gone, both bandages lying in the muddy ditch.

A large crowd was gathering, no civilian authorities. Others were weeping now. Vehicles backed up at both ends behind the accident, not being able to see what the holdup was, started to lose patience, shrill horns, revving engines. I couldn't think. I didn't know what else I could do for the young girl. I was no medic.

My hands started to shake, adrenaline was kicking in. I heard scuffling behind me and turned to see the locals, fortunate enough to be close to their shacks and able to grab something sharp, hacking at the dead horse with machetes, axes, knives of all sizes, even American bayonets. Their first opportunity for fresh meat in days.

Blood from the butchered horse was now mixing with that of the cart driver. His outstretched arm close to a severed hoof, in a ghastly attempt to reclaim what was rightfully his.

Scooters, motorcycles, anything small enough to squeeze by were now doing so, leaving bloody tire tracks in their wake.

Then there was a smell, feces from two relaxed sphincter muscles.

I turned a full circle from the butchered horse to the little girl to the bloody tire tracks to the dead cart driver. I must have looked the total fool.

Praying for wisdom...praying...for something. I started to touch my helmet liner, thinking of my little Bible, and then remembering I no longer carried it...didn't deserve it.

Finally, the sound of a civilian siren.

It was at this point I did something I have spent the rest of my life trying to figure out. Was it because I was so involved in something I didn't need to be involved in, and I wanted proof? Was it to show how unflinching and gutsy I was? Was it to be able to show up at guard mount stained in blood and get away with it? Or was it something much deeper, deeper and darker...some macabre fugue state I was drawn into?

The guy was obviously dead, mouth half open, eyes wide open, a basketball-sized bloodstain on his shirt front. I knelt next to him, ostensibly to make sure he was dead but, to...what? I pressed my right ear to his chest, knowing full well I would get his blood on my cheek and in my ear and hair...trying to.

~~~~~~

Villa Guard

Close to my fourth birthday I was playing by the house, wearing my cowboy hat and plastic six shooters, picking off stage coach robbers. It was windy that day and the lilac bushes behind me were waving in the wind, emitting their distinctive fragrance.

A coal truck came to a stop by the house and the driver asked if I wanted to buy a dog. Being four, I said yes. Mom and Jo came out and he held up this grungy-looking black mutt, saying it's the last one. Now I wanted the puppy even more, feeling he needed a friend.

My sister and mom thought that since dad was back in the Veteran's hospital to stay, I should have a dog. Jo was 16 and working in downtown Schenectady at Kresge's Department store. She and mom pooled their money and bought me the pup.

"It's your dog now, Bobby, what do you want to name him?"

Glancing at the lilac bushes, off the top of my head, I said, "Windy." The way they asked the question, I thought if I didn't name him right away, he wouldn't be my dog.

We brought him inside and gave him a bath. It turned out that a lot of the black was coal dust and he was mostly white. *A real dog and he was mine.*

As I grew older, there was nothing neater than having Windy see me two blocks away and getting all excited, running the whole distance and jumping up on me. *I felt like somebody loved me...even if my dad didn't.*

When Jo turned 18, she moved to the west coast. Brother Les was 14 and living with our sister Doris and her family so he could attend the high school he preferred. Mom, Windy and I were alone in the house.

Someone in the family owned a camp on Lake Champlain. Windy was mostly an outdoor dog, so we asked our neighbor to see that he had food and water while we were at camp.

When we returned after seven days, there was no dog to greet us. No Windy, running excited circles around me, jumping up and down, barking. The neighbors said he'd been gone for three days.

Mom and I split up and walked the neighborhood half the night calling for him, with no results. We sat around the kitchen table full of remorse and guilt; we shouldn't have gone to camp knowing we couldn't bring Windy...neither of us would be able to sleep.

Suddenly, a scratching at the door and whimpering. We both scrambled for the door and swung it open. This grungy, almost black, dog, looking much like he did the day he became mine, slunk in, tail between his legs, head down, still whimpering, like he did something wrong. Why else would we leave him for seven days?

Now you need to understand what a strong woman my mom was. Remember, she fed, housed and clothed six kids on her own before she and dad got back together. She took in laundry, painted house interiors and even hung wallpaper to bring in money for her family. But the night Windy came home, she sat on the kitchen floor hugging the daylights out of that dog and cried her eyes out.

Chapter 23

CAN YOU SAY, "OBNOXIOUS?"

Late one night in September, around 2300 hours, before the villa guard was posted, a white mouse was chasing some *Cowboy* up the gravel road to our villa. The kid ran past the entrance toward the high school and the mouse fired a warning shot.

One thing you could depend on a White Mouse for was to fire his hand gun for no good reason and in the wrong direction. The round hit our Conex, just above our ammo boxes. That woke up an entire villa full of military police. Several of us were now standing outside in various stages of dress, I was in my skivvies. One of the FNGs caught everyone's attention because he was wearing only his steel pot, flack vest and his OD boxer shorts. He was well-armed though, M16 in his left hand, drawn .45 in his right, bobbing and weaving like Barney Fife.

He wasn't in my squad, but a week later this same guy needed a ride back to the villa from the PMO. I was on patrol, so I took the long way back. On Tran Phu, near the toe of the boot, we passed an elderly man on a bike. He caught my eye because his *non-la* (conical straw hat) was secured with a brightly colored scarf under his chin, half orange and half purple with yellow polka dots.

I was watching the road but out of the corner of my eye I saw the man weaving off the shoulder into the bushes. I slowed down and looked back to see if the old guy was okay. He seemed to be, standing next to the bike with this bewildered look on his face.

The FNG was laughing. He said he stuck his nightstick out to try and catch the spokes of the bike's front wheel, hoping to send the guy over his handlebars. "You obnoxious son-of-a-bitch, what the hell's wrong with you?"

He said nothing until we got to the villa. Then he said to Napier, who's headed out on foot patrol, "'Deputy Dawg here says I'm ob," he mispronounced "obnoxious." Jerry looked at me, grinned, rolled his eyes and walked off.

Some guys like Butch Pennelli, Jack Garchow and Jerry Napier were born to be MPs. Some were not. This same guy and I would be at odds again before my tour was over.

~~~~~~

West Gate Guard

They say that during the dance marathons of the 1920s and 30s, people slept while standing up. I was about to prove it.

One Monday I suffered a bad reaction to my Primaquine pill and was up most of the night.

Tuesday, I was stuck on swing shift at the West Gate. The repetitious cadence of the drilling ARVNS was putting me to sleep. *"Một hai ba bôn, một hai ba bôn."* I thumbed the strap of my M16 and shrugged it off my shoulder. Putting the butt on the ground in front of me, both hands resting on the barrel, feet apart, knees locked I made a tripod of sorts.

A quick whoop, whoop of a siren and laughing.

"What?"

"What do you mean, what? You Rip Van Winkle or something? I pulled up here almost a minute ago and you ain't twitched."

Good thing it was Shanker and not some officer...sort of. When I got back to the villa I was greeted with "Hey, what's happening, Rip?"

Okay, let's see. I got dumped on by a female monkey. I woke up with toilet paper wrapped around my ankle. On conny I dropped my rifle in the mud in front of my lieutenant. I mistook ground beef for a traffic fatality. And now, I fell asleep in a position previously not considered possible.

That's five screw ups, but who's counting? One more screw up was yet to come.

~~~~~~

Villa Guard

Barrel-chested and 5'9", Ed Weld was my mom's sister's husband. Navy tattoos on his bristly forearms, thinning hair and big hands. Although not Italian, he always reminded me of a Mafioso. His fondness for fedoras and trench coats completed the image.

When my aunt died, he asked mom if she would move to his place further up-state near Saratoga to be his live-in housekeeper. He said that she and I would share his spare bedroom. Windy would come with us and then Weld added what a great kid he always thought I was.

Mom was back to wallpaper hanging and whatever other chores she could pick up to make a living. So, since we would have free room and board, she could rent out our house in Schenectady and have a steady income. Also, prompted by someone who thought I was a *great kid* sealed the deal.

I wasn't thrilled about all this and my second-grade teacher made a big thing out of me leaving. This only served to make me feel worse. The good news was that my cousin Timi lived next door to Weld's place.

I was seven, she was five, and a fabulous kid. We became remarkably close and did everything together. The only falling out was when my nephew Harold, sister Marge's son, came to visit. At Harold's prompting, he and I ignored Timi for the brief time he was there. Only, when Harold left, I was without my best friend.

A few days later after school as we boarded the bus, resenting my fall from grace and before my lightning fast wit was quite as sharp as it was destined to become, I said, "I smell a skunk nearby." Timi smacked me in the mouth with her lunchbox. Something that was well-deserved, and from which I still bear the scar today, the reason for my mustache.

About two-thirds of the way through second grade, and just starting to make new friends, Weld decided he wanted more than just housekeeping from my mom. So, she and I moved back to the Schenectady house, and I went back to my original second grade class.

Then Weld decided he couldn't live without my mom's expert housekeeping skills, so he promised to remain celibate if she returned. So back we went, back to Saratoga.

Chapter 24

DIGGING A DEEPER HOLE

Because of where we were...thousands of miles from home in a totally different country that was so foreign from anything we ever experienced...what was required and expected of us, and what we confronted every day (there were no routine days for a MP), most of us just didn't care about God or man's laws anymore, what I call the *Fog of War*. Especially when it came to fidelity toward girls back home, be they a girlfriend, fiancé or wife.

We even cheated on the women we were cheating with. Of course, cheating on a prostitute may not count unless you consider her promise not to sleep with any other MP.

I spent two separate nights, not at the villa or Mai's, but at the Rex with girls vacationing in Vung Tau from Saigon. In both cases, it was bewildering to me how a woman with family and friends in a city full of the enemy, destroying hotels like the Victoria and killing Americans...including MPs, could just blow all that off and go man hunting for "tall American Military Policemen" in Vung Tau, one of them actually told me as much. But of course, that didn't stop me either...*Fog of War*.

It gets worse. After one of our drinking marathons at the Beachcomber, three of us decided we wanted to try something new...or more accurately, someone new. It was after curfew and we were using a unit Jeep, so we went to a part of town where we figured the MP vehicle wouldn't be spotted by one of our NCOs. It was a run-down area, but a great place to hide the Jeep.

Within two days, at the start of our work cycle, all three of us came down with gonorrhea. Since an MP's responsibilities wait for no man, we were made to go to the dispensary that morning in full MP kit to get our double shots in the gluteus maximus. We didn't think it was anywhere near as funny as I'm sure that Air Force medic did. The pathetic thing was, we bragged about *getting the clap*, because it underscored our manly risk-taking MP personas...*Fog of War*.

In the four days out of the next fourteen that I saw Mai Lynne, all we did was watch TV. Interestingly, she never questioned my temporary abstention. All things considered, she probably guessed, *Fog of War*.

The reception on Mai Lynne's 9" black and white TV left much to be desired. She could only pick up one station until I jerry-rigged a coat hanger and a sheet of aluminum foil to make an antenna. Even then it was only two channels, and just barely.

Not that it made much difference since the shows were all 1950s American TV reruns: *Father Knows Best, The Adventures of Ozzie and*

Harriet, or *The Adventures of Superman* starring George Reeves. They say Reeves lived in constant fear of someone shooting him to see if bullets would really bounce off his chest. After our television binge, I often thought of George when I was supposed to wear my flack vest. Another show, *I Love Lucy,* had a real international flavor: Cubin-accented Desi Arnaz dubbed in Vietnamese with French subtitles.

~~~~~~

Villa Guard

We were back in Saratoga for the rest of second grade and the first half of the third. It was at this point that Windy disappeared. Getting off the school bus one day, he wasn't there to greet me. When I asked mom where he was, Weld said "he ran off," with such finality I didn't dare question him. I looked back at mom and she just turned away.

About this time Ed decided the only way to end the celibacy issue was to propose. Why mom said yes has been a family debate for years ... still is. She raised all her kids alone and now she wanted ... indeed, deserved, a strong, decisive helpmate for at least part of her life. My dad, with all his problems, was not the one. So, Ed Weld filled that need. That's my take on it.

Unfortunately, Ed's next issue turned out to be me. He decided mom cared more about the son of her first love then she did for him. Consequently, that meant he mostly ignored me or directed outbursts of anger at mom when he'd come home from drinking after work. He always needed to prove his definition of "manliness."

When he wasn't pointedly ignoring me or yelling at mom, he'd regale us with his barroom exploits, how he'd backed down everyone in the bar that disagreed with him. He was sensitive about the fact that during his time in the Navy there was no war for him to win.

My mother was not the type to take a lot of abuse, even verbal. So, we were always leaving. But he was good at luring her back with promises of no more drinking and being a better father to me.

At one point he built a house for her near my sister Margie and another time bought one back in Schenectady. Consequently, between the start of second grade and the end of fifth we moved seven times.

The reason we left the house Ed built was the reason he never laid a hand on me. I was playing outside in the snow with Harold, and my mittens were soaked through. I came to the kitchen door to get some dry ones. Mom said, "Come in and warm up while I look for another pair."

But Weld, who was drinking in the living room, said "He can stay outside. He'll drip all over the floor."

"No, he's cold, let him warm up."

I stepped into the kitchen. She started for my room to get some mittens and Ed started for me. As he staggered toward the kitchen, mom grabbed the neck of the five-pound metal horse statue sitting on the TV and raised it up over her head.

"If you touch my son, I'll kill you."

He sat back down.

~~~~~~

Jimmy Wick's BB gun arrived in mid-October. Our squad, as de facto owners, got to decide just who on the other squads got to use it when on graveyard shift. The most popular bartering tools were cigarettes or buying rounds for our squad at the Rex or Beachcomber.

When it was our turn on graves, the two-man mobile patrol used it. Unless duty called, we'd try to hang out near where the outdoor market was set up during the day. The food scraps were our rat bait after midnight.

The Jeeps came equipped with cat eye lenses which we used in blackout conditions instead of headlights, so we used them to sneak up on our victims. We'd take turns driving as the guy riding shotgun zeroed in on our diminutive enemy. This satisfied Wick's bloodlust even more than trying to run them over. Especially when you hit the rat in its' butt and it did a complete back flip with a twist. *Definitely rat payback time.* As I recall, only one shop window fell victim to our midnight marauding.

Naturally, we soon dubbed ourselves the *Rat Patrol*. Although we didn't realize it at the time, just a month before Jimmy got his gun, a television show of that same name, starring Christopher George and Claudine Longet started its two-year run back in the States. However, the real irony was that Ms. Longet's and my paths would cross a decade later when I was a police officer in Aspen, Colorado.

Chapter 25

TWICE AS PARANOID

Lieutenant Latham rotated out and his replacement, Second Lieutenant Whitlese, felt it necessary to emphasize the extreme importance of my next Top Secret security run to Saigon, this time to MACV. I stood there at parade rest while he detailed the full kit I was to wear which, of course, I already knew, having made the run in June. But the MACV destination got my attention.

It was just over-enthusiasm on the part of our new second looie, but such succinct emphasis on the armament I would need to carry and the use of the words "Top Secret" more than once, plus the drop-off point made my imagination work overtime and made me a little apprehensive.

The ride via military bus from Tan Son Nhut to Saigon seemed to take forever this time. The longer it took, the more uptight I got. *Just because you're paranoid, doesn't mean they're not out to get you.*

Just as I started to relax, knowing that the insane traffic meant I was in the city and close to my destination, I slammed against the seat in front of me. The bus came to a complete stop and the door hissed open. From the window I heard agitated Vietnamese voices and saw people running helter-skelter.

Now I could smell a mixture of gasoline and tear gas. Even the civilian cops were involved, blowing whistles, frantically waving their arms. All this plus Lieutenant Whitlese's pointedly over-cautious briefing made me think there was an extraordinarily strong possibility that this did indeed involve the top secret dispatches I carried.

I instinctively drew my .45 and chambered a round. Thinking twice, I holstered it again and grabbed for my M16 that was leaning against the bench seat. But the sudden stop had slid it under the seat in front of me and out of sight. With my heart in my throat, I went for my .45 again. Thinking better of it, I again went after the M16.

My right hand gripped the back of the seat in front of me and with my chest pressed against it, I groped blindly with my left hand. Webbing...a strap! I grabbed it with two fingers and my thumb. It's a canteen strap. I shoved it under the seat behind me and tried again. More webbing, I slid my fingers slightly to the right, the hard steel of a rifle barrel. *Thank God!*

The M16 had a three-position fire mode selector switch on the left side. I brought the rifle to my chest and thumbed it from safety through semi to full automatic. I slid to the left side of my bench seat and put the rifle to my shoulder, hunkered down behind the seat in front of me. I sensed movement to my rear and turned to see a Marine lance corporal crossing the aisle and taking the same position on the other side of the bus. He apparently felt like he needed to defend the bus from being boarded as well.

Heart pounding, I ran what I knew about the enemy's weapons through my head: the Chinese version of a Russian AK47 held a 30-round banana clip. My M16 held 20. I did have another clip duck taped to the one loaded for "quick-flip" insertion. But a M16 can empty a clip in three seconds. I needed to take care...there may be more than one trying to board. Then I remembered I only have 17 rounds in each clip because M16s tend to jam if you put too much pressure on the feeder-spring, making it his 30 rounds to my 34 with a very rapid "quick-flip" after the first 17.

I glanced back at the Marine. He had the "thousand-yard-stare" -- *he's been in the bush*. I was really happy to have a Marine on my side instead of against me in some bar.

Now I thought, *oh Lord, maybe they'll use a rocket-propelled grenade,...but that would be hard to conceal, and it would risk destroying the dispatches they were after.*

Now came the smell of more gasoline and teargas with more screaming in Vietnamese. I blinked hard, trying to clear the sting and blur of sweat in my eyes. An arm moved through the haze, blocking my view of the dashboard...*they're boarding*. I re-seated the rifle stock on my shoulder and moved my index finger from the guard to the trigger. But then I saw that the arm had moved from the driver's seat to the door, not the other way around. The hand attached to the arm grabbed a handle, the door hissed closed and the bus lurched forward.

Two blocks later, the driver announced, "MACV."

My heart jack-hammered as I walked to the front of the bus. The Marine barked, "What the hell...what was all that shit?"

Driver, pulling the door lever inward, "Beats me, ask inside."

As we walked between two sandbagged bunkers on either side of the door, each with a heavily armed MP and QC, I said to the Marine: "You get the feeling our driver was used to that crap?"

"Yeah."

Because of the locked security satchel, without having to ask, I was directed to a full bird colonel's office. He had just slammed down his phone, obviously not in a good mood. I guessed that the call was about whatever happened down the street. So I chose to stand at attention rather than parade rest. He unlocked the satchel, quickly thumbed through the contents and waved me off with the back of his hand.

I held my salute for a few seconds before he snapped one back without looking up.

I heard myself say, "Begging your pardon, Sir, do you know what that commotion was down the street?"

"No."

The tone of that one syllable word spoke volumes, *yes, but I'm not talking to you about it.*

I gave one more embarrassed salute (this one unanswered) and left. *I can't believe I said "begging your pardon Sir," like some old war movie!*

As I walked between the two bunkers, I remembered that I was carrying a loaded M16 set on fully automatic. I turned around, went into one of the bunkers, slid the strap off my shoulder and clicked the selector back to safe.

Since I'm standing there with two surprised MPs, I asked if they heard what happened down the street.

The American MP said, "Some Buddhist monk doused himself with gasoline and lit a match."

The QC said "He no like treatment."

I didn't know what that meant. I glanced at the American who just shrugged.

Wanting to call my wife and mom, after asking directions, I walked several blocks to the USO because I wasn't sure I was supposed to ride a Lambro with a rifle and sidearm in Saigon.

Once again, the lines were so long we had to limit our phone calls to one. I also noticed that I was the only person in the USO under arms (carrying a weapon), and I was called right away to a phone, it must have been the MP brassard.

"Hi, it's me, over."

"Bob? Where are you? Am I supposed to say 'over'?"

"I'm at the USO in Saigon. I just delivered a top...they sent me to Saigon with mail...yes, you're supposed to say over ... um, over." *I hate these calls.*

"I think we should name the baby soon, I'm due in early December, over."

"Yes, I've been thinking about that. I like Rob, short for Robert, like on the *Dick Van Dyke Show*? His character is Rob Petrie but it's short for Robert, I think. If it's a girl, Rob also, but short for Robin, over."

"I can't hear you well, over."

"How much did you ...?"

"You said something about Dick Van Dyke?"

"Listen, I'll write as soon as I get back to Vung Tau. There's a long line here, over."

"Okay, I ..."

"Me too. Bye." *Yet another stellar phone conversation.*

On the bus back to Tan Son Nhut, I sat behind the same driver. He said the Buddhists did that a lot, something about religious equality. "Then why did you slam on the brakes and open the door?" (He was wearing an Air Force uniform and reminded me of "little sum' bitch" back in Vung Tau).

"I wanted to make sure."

Are you serious...FUBAR (fouled up beyond all repair)! It was fortunate, however, I didn't see it, since the sight of a self-immolation was not something I wanted etched into my psyche forever. I'd already seen enough death, with yet one more to come.

On the single prop plane ride back to Vung Tau, my thoughts went back to the short conversation with my wife. Why shouldn't my kid be named after me? I did give him or her my last name, right? And I was, of course, acting like such a stellar future dad. Yeah, sure. Another good reason to have removed that little Bible from my helmet liner.

~~~~~~

Villa Guard

It took the purchase of the house in Schenectady for Weld to win mom back this time. We lived on Westside Avenue from most of fifth grade to the middle of tenth. I reunited with all my pre-second grade buddies and times weren't bad, we all joined Boy Scouts.

Every Tuesday night we'd walk home down Helderberg Avenue from the troop meeting at Fishers' church, looking for our favorite crack in the asphalt that stretched from shoulder-to-shoulder, so we could stand three on either side, stooped over like the crack was a cable laying across the road and we were about to pull it taut. When a car came by we'd yell "PULL," and the car would come to a screeching halt and we'd all run. (This was two hours after reciting the Scout oath.)

It was during these 5½ years that my brother Ernie took his wife's life and then his own. Mom almost died from bleeding ulcers. Back in those days I believed the Lord answered prayers and mom did recover.

~~~~~~

When I was 15 years old, sitting in the kitchen, I heard and then saw Ed and mom arguing in the dining room, or rather, Ed shouting and mom standing there. After just so much of it she headed toward the kitchen and me. This made him furious, he caught up and shoved her so hard she cracked the kitchen drywall with her shoulder. "Don't you ever walk off on me, Edna!"

Soon after, mom and I moved into a single-family home on Green Point Avenue. It's only about five miles from the Westside Avenue house, so for once I didn't have to change schools.

~~~~~~

It's weird how some things you think should frighten you, don't, and things that shouldn't, do. Presuppositions play a big part in it, as with that last top-secret security run to MACV.

We all heard about what happened right in Vung Tau during the French-Indochina war. High ranking French officers gathered at a restaurant to discuss strategy. The Vietminh (Communist-led forces of the 1940s and 50s) attacked and killed all of them, at least that's how we heard it.

So now there is to be a strategy meeting of high ranking officers from all the Allied forces, including General Westmoreland, South Vietnamese Prime Minister Nguyen Cao Ky and others. Not at a restaurant, but at a large building on the outskirts of town and backed up to the jungle. I pulled walking guard duty on the jungle side. I thought it was careless of them to use only one MP from the 560th to guard all this brass but I'm just a Spec 4, what do I know?

My head is full of images of butchered French officers sprawled over bloodied tablecloths and overturned chairs. My only illumination is from the cone-shaped beam of my Army flashlight. I'm scared witless, more so than I ever was entering a bar full of drunk military or merchant marines. I mean, at least those were supposedly good guys. This was the enemy I could be confronting here...Viet Cong.

It's windy, so I was seeing movement everywhere. Then I hear a whistle and I immediately recall some Marine telling me the enemy sometimes blows whistles when attacking in the dark.

Now, definite movement off to my left, low to the ground, but moving fast. I flick off the flashlight and drop it as I swing my M16 from right shoulder arms to my left hand after flicking the safety from semi-auto to full.

An American southern accent, "Rico, still."

Three feet in front of me a military police guard dog comes to a skidding halt, followed by an apologetic MP with a whistle around his neck. The dog had snapped his leash, so the MP grabbed it by the collar. It turned out that all this brass brought their own MPs and guard dogs. He told me there were a half dozen MPs with dogs stationed at various distances in the jungle.

The brass is not as stupid as I thought. Except for the part where no one told me. FUBAR

Chapter 26

SWAG

Main Gate

Occasionally, the generosity of other units proved to be advantageous to us, especially at the gates. Rarely did a commissary or mess hall truck enter through the main gate without giving the duty MP some food or drink.

Sometimes hard liquor (hence the infamous MP drink, catalyst to the great toilet paper legend) but usually C rations (a complete pre-cooked canned individual meal) which were last made in 1953 but nonetheless ended up in our war and our town. If it was good enough for Korean war soldiers, it was good enough for us.

We didn't care how old they were, only that they were free and more or less edible. There were six single meal ration boxes per cardboard case. They consisted of:

- A meat entrée, which could be chopped eggs and ham or pork and beans or *mystery-meat* chunks and beans;

- One of three bread components, labeled, B-1, 2, or 3:

    - B-1 contained a cocoa disc and a 1.5 oz. tin of jam;

    - B-2 boasted one cookie sandwich and a chocolate fudge disc; and

    - B-3 held two cookie sandwiches and a 1.5 oz. tin of jam.

- Five crackers.

- A packet of instant coffee.

- Powdered milk.

- A packet of granulated sugar.

The rest varied:

Just to confuse everyone, there was also a B-4 unit. The bread component was none of the above but a packet of pre-mixed and compressed cereal.

All contained a 12-ounce can of fruit, gum, toilet paper [a pathetically small amount], a P-38 can opener, a granulated salt packet, a flat wooden spoon and a cigarette packet which had one 9-pack of cigarettes and a book of matches. The cigarettes were always packed so tight they looked like 5" long rectangles.

The type of B unit was marked on each of the six boxes and we all had our favorite, so the MP on the gate would pull his box out before bringing the other five to the villa.

Once a sergeant from signal corps gave me two cases. So, seeking to surprise her, I brought one to Mai, but she failed to see why one would want to eat 13-year old food in little green cans, boxes and packets. I guess she had a point, nonetheless after pulling a B-2 unit with the one cookie sandwich and chocolate fudge disc out of the case, I brought the rest to the villa.

Another freebie we received was #10 cans of recombined chocolate milk. There was also a white milk version, but it tasted like chalk. Most of the units knew we preferred the chocolate, so that's all they'd drop off. The chocolate didn't taste much better than the white, but it was the closest thing to real milk we could get.

Since there was only one refrigerator, all these cans ended up in there, but the entire platoon had access. We hung a church key on the door handle of the fridge to punch two holes in the can and we all drank out of whichever one was open.

Chapter 27

Bread and Circuses

"Staff Sergeant, you were going 35. The speed limit in the whole town is 20 miles per hour."

Gravelly southern accent, "Yeah...I'm in a hurry."

"And why is that?"

"Maybe I'm late making extra sandwiches for you guys." He was the mess sergeant from one of the units on the airbase and was reminding me he provided us with food on graveyard shift, *snotty attitude*.

He actually stuck a cigar in his mouth while I stood there, raising a tattooed forearm to light it. *It's the same sergeant from my first morning at the Fort Dix induction center, sticking his head out the mess hall window, giving us that 20-minute orientation after first calling us "little Pussies" and laughing as we dropped like flies.*

I said, tossing the ticket in his lap, "Tell you what, read this while you're burning our toast."

Our first graveyard shift after I gave that staff sergeant his citation, Napier on the PMO desk called in a food request. As we stood there, we could barely hear the voice on the other end, but we all heard someone in the background:

"Is that the MPs?"

Muffled voice, "Yes, sergeant."

"Tell them we're too busy."

The next night Sergeant Cooper called and we all heard: "MPs?"

Muffled voice, "Yes, sergeant."

"Give me the phone." Then, "Cooper?"

"This is Sergeant Cooper...yes?"

"One of your people has a real bad attitude."

I knew that was coming, so when sarge looked up, my hand was already raised. A few more words we couldn't hear and then sarge looked at me, shook his head, and said, "I'll handle it, sergeant."

Cooper hung up the phone and said, "Fix this, Bob."

Since Sergeant Cooper put it that way instead of using my rank (as in, *fix this specialist*) I felt we'd both taken a mutual dislike to that mess sergeant. That gave me the impetus to *fix this* quickly and, in a way not expected.

I went to the unit of the guy I pulled out of the alley by Mai's place. After checking on him, I spoke to his sergeant (being sure to remind him of who I was by mentioning how hard it was getting all that blood out of my .45 ammo clip) and then I asked if he would come with me to talk to his mess sergeant.

That third day of graves we gained a new source of late night food and I got to eat sandwiches, instead of crow.

~~~~~~

Villa Guard

By November 1960, mom started reminding me of things like Weld first asking her to move in as his housekeeper and saying what a great kid I was. Then she added how when he and her sister used to visit us, he thought it was so cute when I would climb up on his lap and play with the zipper on his shirt, accidently catching the hair on his chest.

Of course, that was all bull on his part. If I did that after he and mom were married, he would have knocked me across the room, if not for mom and her five-pound metal horse.

Being 15, I realized all this meant that if he asked her back, she would go. But in February 1961, my concern ended abruptly. The police showed up at our door and told us that Weld was dead.

His hunting buddy discovered him on the kitchen floor, dead from heart issues. Ironically it was in the same room he shoved my mom into the wall.

Les asked me how I felt about Weld dying. I just shrugged and said nothing. I was thinking about the time he told me to go to the store and pick him up a loaf of bread. Knowing that he couldn't stand fresh bread, I spent his money on the softest loaf I could find. I was delighted when I heard the screen door slam and saw him storming off to get another loaf. The loaf I got him was balled up and tossed in the kitchen trash.

Now I felt guilty.

~~~~~~

Lately, my six kids wouldn't follow me all the way to the candy store if they spotted an orange-robed Buddhist monk. They'd break off and follow him, thinking maybe he would set himself on fire. Death was more exciting than candy. Even for little children.

Chapter 28

THE SHOOT-OUT

In November I received a letter from my nephew Bud. He's in the Navy as an electronic technician with the rank of E-5 on the USS Henrico, repairing radio and radar equipment. Henrico's mission was to carry reinforcements and replacements from Okinawa and the Philippines to various bases in south Vietnam.

Bud wrote, "We're stopping at several ports along the coast to disembark Marines. On the 15th the stop is Vung Tau, the in-country R&R center. I plan on finding the E-club (enlisted men's club) and consume copious amounts of 'Tiger beer.'" Due to the complicated Army post office addressing system he didn't realize that's where I was stationed.

He continued, "I want to forget this 'crossing' entirely. Picture your poor nephew climbing to the top of a radar mast while the ship is underway because the captain needs to find the beachhead to land the Marines. That's why some of the old Bos'n mates call us 'twidgits.' I think its Navy slang for *nerd*."

It was just my luck that I was on static post that day at the main gate rather than walking or driving wherever I pleased. As soon as the MP from the next squad relieved me at the end of swing shift, I jumped into his Jeep and sped to the plateau in full MP kit. No 30 drunken sailors this time, just a couple shore patrol and five drunken sailors.

I asked if anyone knew if the Henrico was in port. Two guys spoke up, not the SPs, they just looked annoyed.

"Do you guys know Bud ... Joe Holtslag?"

Sailor number one "Who?"

"Bu...Joe Holtslag."

Sailor number two "What?"

"Joe, Joe Holtslag!"

Sailor number one "I think his tour was up and he went home."

"What ... um ... no, I got a letter ... could he be in town?"

Sailor number one "Maybe, but I have no idea where he lives."

Sailor number two "Seattle, wasn't it?"

I hear the two SPs laughing. I turned to them, "Do you guys know Joe Holtslag?"

"Not sure, is he from Seattle?" *cute*. Now everyone's laughing.

I was tempted to unsnap my holster but opted to tell the group as a whole "If he shows up, would you tell him his Unc"...*Don't go there,* "his friend is looking for him? That I'm an MP stationed here?"

Sailors one and two "Gee, no shit."

~~~~~~

Villa Guard

"Hey Unc, it's Bud. I got the new scope for my .22, let's go up by Watervliet Reservoir, sight it in and go shoot frogs along the railroad tracks."

"Okay."

"I'll pick you up."

It was Saturday, May 20, 1961, just before my 16th birthday.

Bud brought along a paper target. We taped it up on a wooden box attached to a metal structure along the tracks. He fired half a dozen rounds, adjusting elevation or windage after each shot.

Bud, "What do you think?"

I took a shot, "Looks good to me."

We then walked off to the marshy fields next to the tracks and started our usual frog massacre. Thirty minutes later we saw some railroad employee checking out the box we used to secure the target. We must have been high on marsh gas or something, because we didn't put two and two together.

Fifteen minutes after that, the same guy showed up with a Schenectady County Deputy. That's when we decided to mosey off in the opposite direction. We decided to not run, figuring he might shoot us in the back, but stopped at once when the deputy called to us.

On the way to the County jail, where the Sheriff's office was located, we're in the back of the deputy's cruiser whispering franticly in each other's ear.

"We can say we didn't do it."

"What if they trace the bullets?"

"Or hook us up to a lie detector?"

"Or shoot us up with 'truth serum'?"

It turned out we had destroyed a coil on a signal relay box for the main line of the New York Central Railroad system, holding up trains across New York for five hours.

If all this had happened the next Saturday, it would have been on my open police record file for all to see; including whatever governmental agency investigates the criminal history of potential military police for the United States Army.

Granted, I didn't commit an act of treason or a heinous felony, but my understanding was that the MPs let nothing slide in their security clearance screening. Yet I ended up with top secret security clearance.

What path would my tour of Vietnam have taken if I wasn't an MP in Vung Tau?

How would this memoir read?

Would I even be here to write one?

Was it the hand of God?

Chapter 29

DIMINUTIVE ENTREPRENEURS

It never ceased to amaze me how clever and enterprising Vietnamese kids were. After a pounding rainstorm would splatter mud all over our Jeeps and turn low-lying fields into small ponds, they'd gather in groups of three or four alongside the road wildly waving rags, trying to entice us to back the Jeep into the water, so they could wash them for 5¢ or 10¢.

Kids would wander in and out of the local bars, asking if we wanted anything from the sidewalk pushcarts, hoping for tips if they fetched it for us as well as a gratuity from the cart owner.

When squads held evening beach parties, we buried half of a 55-gallon drum in the sand and filled it with ice and beer. Kids would get wind of the parties and offer to dig the holes, even providing their own shovels (usually stolen entrenching tools). They'd also fetch and open beer for us with church keys hanging around their necks, all for a small fee.

During the day at the beaches, kids would haul around wicker baskets, bigger than they were, full of pineapples. In less than five minutes if you gave them 5¢ they'd carve a spiral from stem to tip removing all the burrs and skin and leaving just the juicy yellow pulp. One could eat everything but the stem. Of course, the citrus content would make your lips smart. If you made a face and licked the corners of your mouth, they thought it was funny.

The most fascinating thing they did was fish in open gutters next to a culvert pipe with a 3-4' long stick with 5' of string attached to it and an open safety pin on the other end with a scrap of food on it and within seconds they'd pull up a fat bullfrog for supper.

A 16-year old boy named Bi`nh (one of several first names used by both sexes, which meant *peace* or *peacefulness*), ran a bustling horse and buggy business, usually catering to GIs on R&R trying to impress Vietnamese women.

He was a nice kid who spoke English fairly well and was always asking about America and what my life was like back there. Also, he was as honest as the day is long. I lost my wallet during one of the squad's three days off parties.

While on mobile patrol my first time back on day shift and stopped at an intersection, I heard "Bob Schuse, Bob Schuse." (Why do Asians have such a tough time with my last name?)

It's Bi`nh, running down the sidewalk and reaching for his hip pocket at the same time. He stops at my Jeep, all breathless and out comes my wallet. I didn't even remember riding with him the night of the party.

Not wanting to do it in front of him; after he caught his breath and walked back to his buggy, I counted the money in my wallet. All $40 were there. That would have been enough to buy a new horse.

The fact that he thought Mai Lynne was beautiful didn't hurt either. My first ride in his cart was with Mai...looking as stunning as usual. The second time I was alone.

Bi`nh said: "You love lady friend?"

"Well..."

"Cô ấy đẹp."

I nodded, "Yes, she is beautiful."

~~~~~~

Bar girls were certainly an enigma. They dressed nice in ao dais or American-style skirts or dresses, but never outrageously, like hookers. They wore minimal makeup with their raven hair at various lengths, usually straight.

A lot of the girls were married or had Vietnamese or American boyfriends. Their job was to sit with the guys, just talking and keeping them company.

The GIs spent lots of money getting totally loaded and buying Saigon Tea for their companions, nothing but shot glasses of Kool-Aid or actual tea, which could be quickly consumed. The girls split the cost of the tea with the bar owner. At $2 a pop, it was quite profitable.

I equated the entire system to the taxi dance halls of the 1920s and 30s. Instead of paying 10¢ for a ticket to dance with a girl, you'd pay $2 to sit at a bar with one.

At closing time, the girls would excuse themselves and leave, dashing all hopes of a more intimate ending to the evening. That's why the bar girls really liked the MPs, we kept the bars safe, especially at closing time since we were the buffer between them and the frustrated GIs.

Consequently, when we were off-duty, we could talk to them all we pleased without buying Saigon Tea. The owners said nothing, as it was their bars we were protecting.

After work, the girls would go home to their husbands or boyfriends. Often, if it was an American, the two would chip in for a place to live, or the girl would pay for it herself if she was making enough money, which was usually the case.

One bar girl had the most delightful giggle and the goofiest sense of humor. She changed her name every time she changed bars, picking a Vietnamese name that sounded the most like a numerical equivalent in English. When I left, she was working at the Melody bar and up to the number three (phonetically "Twee," in Vietnamese).

Some of the single or unattached girls would return to the bars after closing and sleep in the back room.

~~~~~~

Villa Guard

By summer's end 1961 (just before starting 11th grade), who bought the Westside house from mom? My cousin Timi's parents!

So Timi and I got to end our school days the same way we started them, going to the same school. Fortunately, Mohonasen High provided food service so there was no need for Timi to be armed with a lunchbox.

She was so extroverted, personable and good looking, she fit in immediately. Also, she quickly made cheerleader.

Me? Not so much. More than once a couple of guys said to me they couldn't believe Timi and I were cousins, we were so different.

In retrospect, I realize that after all the moving and changing of schools, I simply gave up on the idea of trying to make new friends. What was the point?

I just stuck with the guys I knew since early childhood. I didn't have a brother close in age or any real father figure to help me cultivate any confidence or even coach me on how to throw a baseball or swing a bat, so of course I wasn't into sports, which was obvious.

Amazingly, as well as Timi coming back into my life, mom got married again, to her other deceased sister's husband.

She said, "Bobby, you're only 16 and still need a father." *I could have done without the last two.* Of course, she was really asking if I would mind if she married again and did I remember Hanna's husband, Bill? And what a nice guy he was?

I knew she genuinely felt I should have a dad (she asked Les to teach me how to shave) and she still desperately needed a strong decent life partner, even at 61 years of age. She deserved one.

"I remember," I said, lying.

As it turned out, Bill Crounce was a great guy. He cherished my mom, never raised his voice, only scolded me when I needed it, or to back up mom. I'd always wanted a positive male role model. I finally had one.

With renewed confidence and no fear of moving and starting all over again, my social life improved immensely. Although not playing sports, I attended all the games, went to three formals and graduated with lots of signatures and nice things written in my senior year book.

All's well that ends well.

I won a couple scholarships, regular Regents and Regents' Veterans because of my father's service-connected disability. A high school friend and I both applied to SUNY (State University of New York) at Farmingdale to major in advertising art and design. (The college also offered a major in Police Science. If only I'd known!)

By the Spring of 1965, I had my Associate degree in hand but wanted to goof off one more summer, so I ended up back in Lake George, the same resort town I spent the previous summer between collage semesters.

I cut my summer frolic short that year, thinking I needed to get my act together with a serious job. I left Lake George in mid-August.

Soon after, thanks to my brother Eddy, who was a supervisor at General Electric, I quickly landed a job in the modular display department for GE.

It only took five weeks for the boredom to set in and I found myself in front of that Army recruiter.

Chapter 30

The next best thing to squad parties at the beach was patrolling the beach in our Jeeps after sunset. In addition to the fun of scattering sand crabs, we got to interrupt amorous liaisons between officers and their nurse girlfriends. We figured, if we couldn't fraternize with the nurses, since they were officers, why should we make it easy for anyone else?

There was no regulation about them parking on the beach after dark, so long as it was before curfew. But it was such a riot drawing close to them using just our cat eye lenses then flicking to full headlights and watching clothes fly everywhere.

~~~~~~

"Hey, what are you...a couple of queers?"

This from two Americans in civilian clothes, one with an eagle, globe and anchor tattoo and the other's forearm emblazoned with *Semper Fidelis*, running from elbow to wrist...in script no less.

They were following a pair of ARVN soldiers, who were doing their best to put distance between themselves and the Americans. I didn't need this! Two drunken Marines intimidating our allies when I was already in a foul mood after *explaining* to some shaved-tail looie (second lieutenant, also drunk) that, even with both of us in uniform, I didn't have to salute him since we were indoors, in a civilian bar to boot!

I knew where this was going since the Marines were prancing along and holding their forearms in front of their bodies, waving limp-wristed hands.

"Knock it off guys!" Not very intimidating, but I was still trying to calm down from my last encounter. They both stopped and turned, one said, "Knock up, who?"

The other, "They're not our type."

This isn't going to be fun...hold it in Shults. Biting my tongue, I attempted to explain that in some Asian cultures, close friends locked pinky fingers while walking. "It's a sign of camaraderie."

Eagle globe and anchor guy, "A sign of what?"

Semper Fi guy, "What are you, their daddy?"

I'd taken enough crap for one night. Stepping closer to *Semper Fi* guy I said, "No, but I'd bet they have 'daddies.'" (A twist on the old joke, how do you tell a soldier from a Marine? The soldier knows who his daddy is.)

They both got it.

The one I stepped toward now took a step toward me and I sensed the other one moving to my rear. They were both shorter than me but lean and athletic. I took a half step to my right lining up our left legs, hand on the butt of my nightstick, leaning forward...the rim of my helmet liner nearly touching his left temple.

"Don't even think about it, asshole." *When they push, you have to push back.* Now adrenaline was kicking in.

I heard, "Is there a problem, mate?" It's Bernie, Sergeant Kim and a QC, all jumping out of their Land Rover at the same time. Kim already planted his feet apart, the edge of both of his palms toward the Marines. *Thank God for Koreans and Aussies.*

I said, "It's nothing. Just a misunderstanding," stuffing my shaking hands into my pockets.

Both Marines looked from one MP to the other and quickly nodded agreement. Kim looked disappointed.

Bernie, "Why weren't you down at the corner?"

"You mean besides the obvious reason...these dipshits?"

A nod from Bernie, "Yeah."

"I know where I was supposed to meet you, but I stopped at the Melody bar to say hi to Twee and ran into this tight-assed lieutenant that, ... it doesn't matter, I'm just glad you're here."

~~~~~~

Another unusual Asian custom, more common than adult men locking pinky fingers, was chewing betel nut, like Anh and Thang's grandparents. More accurately, it is an areca nut, the seed of the areca palm wrapped in betel, the leaf of a vine indigenous to Asia. Combined with hydrated lime and sometimes tobacco, it turns the lips dark ruby red and the teeth almost black.

Stranger still, unless one understands the practice, is that of pinching your neck when sick with a cold or sore throat. Squeezing hard enough to leave red welts several places all over the neck.

My friend, Truong (pronounced "Two-ong") or maybe she was calling herself "Twee" at this point, I forgot if she was in her second or third bar at the time, explained that you apply medicated oil to the neck and then you pinch the flesh to make sure the oil sinks deep into the skin. And here I thought it was hickeys from overly enthusiastic boyfriends. When I finally translated that joke into pidgin English, I thought Twee was going to fall off her barstool laughing that insane giggle of hers.

Chapter 31

'TIS THE SEASON

It was getting close to Thanksgiving and we were all anticipating a special meal for the holiday. After all, we had our meals in a hotel, how bad could it be?

It turned out to be pressed turkey, powdered mashed potatoes, cold gravy, and some kind of dried fruit, not cranberries.

However, the highlight of the feast was the active ingredient in the cornbread stuffing. I mean that literally. Tiny black insects. I couldn't see them on the surface. I separated the chunks with my fork to watch them scurry further in, out-of-sight.

I have a problem with cornbread to this day.

Now Christmas was coming. On December 15, 1966, Jimmy lay on an aluminum beach lounger in the villa yard, holding a tri-fold sun reflector to his shirtless torso with one hand, and his transistor radio tuned to the Armed Forces network in the other. Within reach was his BB gun. He knew that sooner or later someone would offer our squad a couple packs of cigarettes in trade for its use on graves that night. Smokes were ridiculously cheap at the PX, nonetheless, what a sweet deal for the six of us!

I held Ho Chi while little Anh patted him on the head. Lately she had been calling us MP and Chi-Chi. Probably because it rhymed. (She's a bright kid and funny like Twee.) For some reason she's counting each pat to Ho Chi's head. Having nothing better to do, I'm counting along with her in English. At 15 I'm amazed at how high she can count for a three-year old.

15...the 15ᵗʰ...suddenly it hits me, "Oh wow! Hey Wicks, I almost forgot. Today starts my last hundred days in-country. I'm officially a 'short timer!' I drew up my FIGMO chart weeks ago."

And to little Anh, "Honey, I gotta go."

"I gotta go put my chart up on my locker and darken the hundredth section."

Sergeant Brown, our new top sergeant, called out from the door of his villa billet, "Shults, you and Wicks will be the first to know. Sometime in January, elements from first platoon are moving from Bien Hoa to Vung Tau to build barracks for us. We're moving out of town and onto the base."

Then he matter-of-factly added, "Some second platoon personnel will be helping with the construction, so the rest of us are going to 12 on and 12 off."

You could almost hear my bubble burst. And then, waving three envelopes with the familiar red, white and blue air mail markings, "Shults, you missed mail call."

As I headed for the villa and my locker, I held letters from Bailie, my sister Margie and my wife. I opened hers first and started reading. I stopped in my tracks: "Your daughter, Robin Lynne Shults, was born December 2. She has 10 fingers and 10 toes and she's beautiful."

Over the radio I heard, "From Los Angeles, California. Walt Disney dead at 65."

Jimmy, having flung his reflector across the villa yard, is now sitting up "12 on and 12 off? Shit! Shit! Shit!"

From little Anh, "You want Coke?"

I spent Christmas Eve with Mai. Later I heard from the villa guard that no one from my squad spent the night at the villa, all of us staying with girlfriends or chasing skirts at the Rex (I guess that would be chasing ao dai at the Rex).

On Christmas day I was on the main gate 0800 to 1600. I wore a red holiday bow taped to the front of my helmet liner right between the "M" and the "P" the entire eight hours.

The interpreter brought a radio and set it on the window sill of the guard shack tuned to the Armed Forces' channel, blaring holiday songs all day.

At one point, I tried to teach the interpreter to jitterbug to Brenda Lee's *Rocking Round the Christmas Tree.* (During my last two years at Mohonasen, school dances were my life.) Quang, the QC, said, "You funny. Put helmet on her head, she look like turtle dancing with stork."

Chapter 32

CHANGING OF THE GUARD

January 1967. I'd been in-country a little over nine months. A new year, and so many changes. Top Sergeant Greene, Sergeant Raymer and Lieutenant Latham all rotated out, along with two of my buddies, Jack Garchow and Butch Pennelli...long gone.

In my squad, Jerry Napier had gone home to his wife, ceremoniously presenting the rest of his prophylactics to Nate Shanker and Jimmy Wicks. He was replaced by FNG Billy Butler.

True to his word, Sergeant Brown put an entire six-man squad on barracks' building duty with the first platoon guys now living at the Vung Tau airbase.

That left us with just three squads for mobile and foot patrol as well as static post duties, plus convoy and VIP assignments. We did indeed start "12 on and 12 off."

Sergeant Cooper had been a civilian contractor, so Brown put him in charge of the whole building project. Thus, we lost our squad leader. He was replaced by Sergeant Callahan who transferred from another MP company.

Incredibly, but ultimately unfortunate for me, Callahan was from Schenectady. We were familiar with each other's high schools, hangouts, etc. and we met in Vung Tau, Vietnam, 10,000 miles from home.

The problem: Callahan and I never got along. It started with his stupid idea that he never heard of a true Schenectadian who didn't drink beer.

Which wasn't technically correct, in my case at least. I was anchorman on my college dorm beer drinking team (no kidding). I drank beer at squad beach parties, just not at the R&R facilities because of my theory about getting drunker quicker and cheaper on hard liquor. After all, getting loaded off-duty was always my goal, so it made sense to me.

I'd be darned if I was going to start drinking beer whenever the squad got together just because of Callahan. I told him one time in front of the guys that I doubted that being a beer drinker was in the Schenectady City Charter. Everyone else laughed. Things sort of went downhill from there.

About a week into our new shift schedule, two guys from one of the remaining three squads, decided they preferred to build barracks eight hours a day rather than be cops for 12. They went to Top and claimed they had carpentry experience. Whether it was true or not, I don't know, but off they went.

To balance the squads out, Brown had Callahan and Sergeant Hemple each reassign a man to the short squad, Sergeant Stubin's, which gave each squad the same number of men, just five MPs. Not only did our jobs become even harder, but Callahan jumped at the chance to get rid of me.

They let me stay with my friends: Shanker, Wicks and new guy Butler but now I was in the squad with Donnie Wheeler, the guy who liked to jam nightsticks into bicycle spokes and couldn't pronounce *obnoxious*, but worse, it seemed that every time I was on two-man patrol, foot or mobile, I was with him.

How Pennelli would have freaked working with someone as tactless as this guy! *Hearts and minds.*

One day I'm driving on mobile patrol and heard, "Shults, stop. Stop the Jeep!"

We're on Hoang Dieu, so I think there's a situation in a bar. I'm adjacent to the Starlight and the Melody and problems this early in the afternoon are not unheard of but they are rare. I hit the brakes, having been headed toward Front Beach, so the bars are across the street.

The only movement I saw was a young couple coming out of the Starlight. A pretty Vietnamese girl, maybe early 20s, wearing an ao dai, arm-in-arm with a young American sailor in his whites. Her head is on his shoulder...*Mai and me.*

I didn't know what the situation was between the two, but he looked like he had died and gone to heaven. He was looking around to see if anyone noticed his girl. The sailor was about 5'6" and having a beautiful lady that was shorter than him was a plus.

Then Wheeler blocks my view of the couple. They were the reason we stopped. The sailor's cap was still in his belt since he had just come outdoors and hadn't put it back on. Granted he may have been so distracted he would have forgotten altogether.

I would have caught his attention, grinned, pointed to my belt, then tapped my head, but not Wheeler. Hands on the butts of both his nightstick and .45, he's nose-to-nose, like some induction center DI, chewing the kid out.

The sailor is acutely embarrassed and now finds himself with one of two choices, kowtow in front of his lady to this idiot who is way over the top, or get belligerent. He chose the latter.

By the time I crossed the street, the girl was really frightened, having backed up a few steps, eyes wide and both hands over her mouth. The sailor is now leaning into the confrontation, standing on his toes.

I give kudos to the kid. Wheeler was my height with his helmet liner adding another five inches. I saw Wheeler lining up their left legs, hand shifting to the top front of his nightstick. *Did I teach him that?*

I put a hand on each guy's shoulder. Wheeler spun toward me, unsnapping his nightstick and raising it to shoulder height. I had to give him that one. Other than that night at the Nguyen's, I'd never broken up a confrontation where an MP was part of the problem, so I forgot to identify myself before putting my hands on their shoulders.

This is getting way out of control, all over a hatless sailor.

Wheeler blinked hard, as if coming out of a trance; confirming what I thought all along, *this man is dangerous.*

He allowed me to put my hand on the top of his nightstick, slowly lowering it to his side.

I said, "I'm gonna finish this shift on foot, you take the Jeep."

"What about this lump of...?"

"I got this."

Right in front of these two people, "Who are you? Giving me orders?" Hesitating, then "Deputy Dawg?"

He hasn't forgotten.

He added, "We're the same rank!"

I said, "It's called date of rank Specialist!"

He flipped us all the bird and stormed off toward the Jeep.

Wow.

Confrontations like this, pointlessly overblown, continued until eventually I asked Sgt. Stubin to either pair me with someone else or let me patrol alone. (You ask sergeants, you don't tell them.)

He agreed, and I was usually partnered with Bill Stringfellow. Bill and I were there about the same length of time. He knew his stuff. He was calm and patient, unless escalation was needed, then he was very good at handling any situation.

Chapter 33

GOVERNMENT ISSUE

By February, Top Sergeant Brown started getting on our cases for abusing unit Jeeps. "You guys are putting your Jeeps in reverse and then slamming them into first without even coming to a stop. You're grinding gears because you're not fully clutching and you're going through brakes like you do prophylactics."

Aside from our weapons, we didn't take the best care of any government issue equipment. Ironic, since we were also government issue, hence the name *GIs*.

Then Brown said, "If you keep it up, I'm gonna stick you all in the motor pool for a half shift." *What would that be? Half an eight-hour? Or half of a twelve-hour shift?*

He started to turn away, then turned back and added, "So you'll be working 16 on and 8 off!" *Half an eight- hour.*

This set the stone, the boulder, in motion; rolling downhill toward my sixth and biggest screw-up – the one in the cleaning room.

Within a week Sgt. Brown was fed up with us for ignoring his warning. I pulled the second 16-hour shift the day after Wheeler pulled his. That meant 0600 to 1800 hours (six in the morning to six in the evening), all of it on foot patrol.

My shift finally finished. I slipped off my brassard, weapons belt, and helmet liner which I replaced with my fatigue hat. Then I headed to the motor pool.

I didn't know squat about vehicle repair, so I was stuck changing tires and oil the whole four hours. I had eaten nothing since noon with the exception of a C-ration pack. I returned to the villa at 2300 hours, raided the refrigerator for a couple swigs of recombined chocolate milk and then hit the sack.

I was up by 0500 hours, that's less than six hours of sleep, and I started all over again.

I was assigned static post at the main gate. Arriving before sunrise, I was just in time to catch a manmade version, a Napalm dawn, just across the bay on the east side of our peninsula about 10 miles away behind the village of Long Hai.

They're probably clearing jungle. But it made me think about what some Marine zoomie (jet fighter pilot) once told me about Napalm. "You don't burn to death. The Napalm sucks up all the oxygen trying to feed itself and, since your mouth is open, and nostrils are flaring as you scream because of the intense heat, your lungs empty of oxygen in a millisecond, and you suffocate." Just the kind of recall I don't need, being as tired and bummed as I am.

When my relief arrived at 1800 hours, as I climb into his Jeep to return to the villa, he said, "Ho Chi is dead."

"What?"

He relayed what he was told to tell me.

Now I stood under the water tower staring at Ho Chi's water bowl/swimming pool and half-empty food dish, wondering what I'm going to tell Anh, when I hear "MP, Chi Chi."

I turned and she had folded her little 3' frame into a squat as close as she could get to the chain link fence, both skinny arms through the links, one hand holding a Coke for me and the other some mango for Ho Chi.

As I walked toward Anh, wondering what to tell her, I had this mixed image of Ho Chi's tiny hand resting on her wrist as she scratched his belly (as if to say, "don't stop") and my dog Windy, leg twitching as I rubbed his belly.

When I got to the fence she asked, "Where Chi, Chi?"

"He ran away" was what came out. *Great, I'm sounding like Ed Weld.*

As if sensing I was down for more reasons than the loss of Ho Chi, Anh said, "No pay, Coke...okay?"

For once I accepted the free Coke, while I fought the urge to run around the end of the fence, pick her up and hug her.

Exhaustion is often a catalyst for poor judgment as well as a lousy attitude. After eating I thought, *it's about time I clean my .45*, something I normally did right after my shift ended, but its 1800 hours and I just wanted to lie down. So, I left word to have the villa guard wake me an hour early, at 0400, figuring I'd clean it then.

Someone shook my bunk "Get up, Shults. Its 4."

I put on my fatigues, web belt and helmet liner, then took my .45 out of its holster and reached for the seven-round clip on my locker shelf. As I started to insert it, I remembered that I was going to clean the pistol. That was the reason I got up early.

Screw it, I'll clean it tomorrow. I continued inserting the clip, re-holstered the gun, took off my belt and helmet liner, and flopped back onto my bunk.

I awoke with a start at 0500 hours and the first thing I felt was guilt. *I can't let fatigue and frustrations keep me from taking care of my weapon.* Since I was already dressed, I slipped on my flip-flops, snatched my .45 out of its holster, and headed for the cleaning room.

Butler was in there, his disassembled .45 on the table...we nodded. For safety reasons, protocol dictates you always clear your weapon before cleaning it to make sure it's not loaded.

I always left my clip on my locker shelf when I headed for the cleaning room, so I jerked the slide and let it slap back as always, to clear the weapon. No round ejected so there was nothing in the chamber. Good. I held the weapon in front of my right shoulder, point it toward the ceiling and pulled the trigger.

All this before Butler could finish a sentence, "That sounds like the clip is still in your...."

Deafening roar of a .45 caliber semi-automatic fired in a closed, acoustically-perfect room.

Butler ducked, both hands over his head. I stood there dumbstruck, as stucco, brick and mortar settled at our feet.

Butler said something else. I didn't hear it. I just saw his lips move. My weapon was four inches from my right ear.

I stood at attention in front of Lieutenant Whitlese for 20 minutes as he chewed me out, but I couldn't hear a word because of the shrill whistle in both ears.

By the time he's done, Sergeant Stubin has given out duty assignments and everyone in the squad has left, leaving one Jeep in the compound. The lieutenant said, pointing, "Take it and get out of here."

I'm acutely embarrassed and humiliated; *what is wrong with you Shults, pulling a stupid FNG stunt like that?*

I pounded the palm of my hand against the top of the steering wheel all the way down Trung Cong Dinh to Front Beach. I needed time to think and gather my composure. Right then I was useless as a cop.

I took a left at Ha Long and a quick right, stopping at the base of the plateau. Behind it is the path down to the Navy docks. To the right is the path to Mai's beach. Nothing in front of me but the South China Sea.

That's who I need right now, Mai. But sitting cross-legged on her bed, hands on each other's knees and telling her what's been going on and having her say something like *"Mon depute fou,"* although I desperately needed it, was not practical just then.

Besides, something was lurking in the shadows of my mind, hidden in the back of my thoughts. Something I couldn't explain to Mai. Something I didn't want to dwell on...something that I couldn't fully grasp myself. But it scared me half to death. I couldn't, I wouldn't, address those hidden shadows for another 15 months.

I sat there staring eastward toward home, knowing that many GIs experienced a lot tougher things than I did. I made up my mind that I was not going to let increased hours, less manpower, the stupid way Ho Chi was killed, moving out of the villa, or anything else, diminish my ability to do my job. That meant I needed to change my attitude and to regain the enthusiasm I enjoyed my first 10 months in-country.

Soon, two things contributed to help change that bad attitude. Four days later someone else did the same thing in the cleaning room. It somehow helped vindicate me and it proved that our extended hours and work load was affecting all of us.

Shortly after the second cleaning room incident, Sergeant Brown suspended our motor pool duties, I suspect at the behest of Lieutenant Whitlese, whom I just happened to be standing near when the second mishap occurred. We both hurried to the cleaning room and after seeing that no one was hurt, Whitlese glanced at me. It was hard to read his expression, so I just raised my eyebrows slightly.

The second thing, I returned to the villa at the end of a 12-hour shift to see Sgt. Callahan sporting a swollen eye and black and blue left cheek.

"What happened Sarge?"

He ignored me, but Nate sidestepped up to me and said, "We were tossing someone into the drunk tank when he suddenly balked and slugged Callahan in the face." Then he added grinning, "He needs to learn how to duck...maybe that should be in the Schenectady city charter."

Chapter 34

GOODBYES

The end of the third week in February, Sergeant Brown told us we'd be moving to the airbase in six days. "I expect you to 'grab your shit and split.'" That was an infantry expression I'll bet he couldn't wait to use.

Then he told me I needed to get a blood draw and give a urine sample, which surprised me, because that's how they check for sexually transmitted diseases and malaria. It's usually done a week before rotating out and I had a month to go...there were still 30 days left on my FIGMO chart.

It took all six days to find time for the blood draw and urine sample. As I lay on my bunk the last night in the villa, watching the leopard gecko on the ceiling (faded white stripe from head to tail), it occurred to me, *if I'm getting checked for STDs and malaria three weeks early, maybe I'll be rotated out early.* Nate happened to be in the room, so I shared the thought with him.

"It's never happened before, Shultsy. It's just some kind of FUBAR."

Then he added, "I wish it were true. We got here the same day and I was told to 'pee and bleed' too."

The next morning all seven Nguyens (including six-month old baby Dat) were in the middle of their yard looking crestfallen as they watched us load a duce and a half with gear. They realized they were going to lose their lucrative income from the MPs. Ever the entrepreneurs, both Thang and Anh held a Coke in each hand. Poking them through the fence hawking, "Coke? Coke?"

Still thinking it's possible I might be rotating out early, I realized I needed to make some serious goodbyes. I avoided looking at the Nguyens, especially the kids, until a more opportune time when I could be alone with them.

The new barracks on the airbase weren't bad. I loved the smell of new wood. Besides the buildings for the platoon (I was on the second floor), they contained a mess hall and showers...real ones with hot water at the turn of a handle. Not a bad place to spend what I assumed would be my last 3½ to 4 weeks.

Best of all, we went back to full strength. The second platoon guys were released from construction duties, so we returned to three days on each shift and three off.

On what was to be my last graveyard shift on international patrol, after rolling around in the dirt on some unpaved back road because some curfew-violating Aussie didn't like authority figures, Bernie finally got the handcuffs on him and Kim threw him headfirst into the Jeep, almost knocking the QC clear out the other side, and the two of us dusted ourselves off.

I said, "At least that's probably the last time I'm gonna be 'dirt dancing' with some penal colony escapee."

"Why's that mate?"

"I was told to 'bleed and pee' early, so maybe I'll be getting on that big silver bird sooner than I figured. Then I won't have to put up with your ugly ass anymore. Our pet monkey could have slipped on those cuffs faster than you did, and he's dead."

Bernie, "Yeah, well, you can kiss *mon cul.*"

"Tell you what, you can have Twee kiss your ass at the Melody at 1800 hours. We ain't got drunk together since the last time Marshal Dillon threw someone out of Dodge."

Then to Kim I asked, "You coming?"

Kim, "I have shift, but I tell you what, you both slowest white men in Vietnam."

I walked into the Melody just in time to see Twee poke Bernie in the chest with her finger and then as he looked down, she used the same finger to pop him under the nose. She did that to everyone, but Bernie is the only one who kept falling for it.

He was sitting with two other Aussie MPs, both of them apparently having been there longer than Bernie. One was leaning back on his bar stool watching Twee walk away, almost losing his balance, and the other seemed transfixed by the metal fan over his head. Bernie introduced them as Harry and Big Mike. "Just Big for short," Big told me. *Drinking with three Aussie MPs...this should be memorable.*

A couple of hours go by and we're all still drinking. The three of them, beers, and me, scotch and soda, most of mine paid for by Bernie since I may be leaving soon. Just to rattle his chain, I told him, "You know Bern, Twee has the hots for you, that's why she keeps poking you in the nose," when Harry said "Think I can stop that bloody fan with my hand?"

The thing is going so fast its humming, and I could hardly see the blades. But before anyone can share their opinion, he stood on the rungs of his stool and tried. The whole bar heard this twang and he sat back down with a quarter of the nail and an eighth of the tip of his middle finger missing.

He simply sat there and said nothing while we all stared, mouths agape, as the bartender, owner and Twee gathered round.

Then its, "aw bloody hell" as a drop of blood from the fan blade landed in his beer but then he stirred it in with his newly shortened middle finger and downed it. The bartender and owner both shook their heads and, still watching Harry, started to walk away, but walked into each other.

Big is the first to speak, "Wow, like beer and tomato juice."

Bernie, "or V-8."

Then Twee, "More like 'bloody Harry.'" Then laughs so hard her elbow slips off the bar.

I walked to Mai's that night, but I got the pouty head shake, beads pulled to her chin. So I hitched a ride back to the barracks. An hour passed and someone hollered up the steps, "The main gate called, some FNG said there's this beautiful chick on a scooter asking for you and if you don't show up he's going to hop on the back and go AWOL."

It's less than four miles to her place, but that's the furthest I've ever ridden on the back of her Vespa, holding onto 20 inches of waist, at least while that drunk.

All night I thought I should tell her I was leaving in three or four weeks. Maybe even a lot sooner. I completely ignored the fact that I already did my STD blood draw to be back with her. I knew she knew tours were a year long, unless you extended, but she didn't bring it up.

~~~~~~

Main Gate

The first week of March is almost over. I'm on day shift with, as it turns out, the two I worked with on Christmas day. My dance partner, whose name I learned was Tran, whom I dubbed "Tran-the-Nimble" and the other... "Quang-the-Whizzer."

It was about 1400 hours (2pm), a cloudless, bright, sunny day. I could hardly see in so much light, so I started looking for my nifty Army-issue aviator sunglasses.

They're not in my fatigue shirt pocket where they should be, so I quickly patted down my other pockets...not there. I looked everywhere, even by the fence post with the crack in the top, that I haven't gone near since the incident with that nasty xenophobic lizard.

Tran and Quang both look at me like I'm crazy, so I felt an explanation was in order. When I told them that I couldn't find my sunglasses, they looked at me like I'm even crazier than they originally thought.

Beginning to get irritated, I accused them of taking my aviators. Tran and Quang looked at each other. Tran turned away her whole body shaking with laughter and Quang said, "Hey, look, I find," as he reaches up and touches the aviator sunglasses I've been looking through the whole time.

That was the last day shift. Then three of swings and three graves, so six more days passed without getting to say my goodbyes, because Mai is no longer six blocks away, or the Nguyens just across the yard.

On the first of my three off there's a Jeep available, so I drove to the villa. As I pulled up I saw Anh in their yard playing with Dat. As I'm parking she shouts, *"Mẹ ngoại ông ngoại đến đây* Bob Shrol...*đến đây."* Mother, grandmother and grandfather do indeed come out, Thang close behind.

I said, "I go America soon. I wanted to say goodbye, um, *Tạm biệt.*"

Grandmother looked at grandfather and they nodded to each other. Grandmother said something to their daughter that I didn't understand. Then the mother said the same thing to Thang.

At this point Anh whirled on her mother, put her little fists on her hips and stomped her foot (much like her performance if you broke a glass Coke bottle).

Thang ran inside and returned with something wrapped in a white rag secured with twine. He is halfway to me when Anh dashed toward her brother, losing both flip-flops, and snatched the item out of his hands. Then she handed it to me, wearing that big grin of hers. I say, *"Cảm ơn bạn,* Anh," as I untie the twine and unfold the cloth. She retrieved her flip-flops, hopped around in the process but without taking her eyes off me. Inside are several pieces of dried squid. I looked up and everyone was wriggling their fingers from half cupped hands.

I thanked everyone again, addressing the elder Nguyens first. They bowed, and I bowed back. Next the kids' mother touched my hand. As I turned, she hugged me and whispered *"Cảm ơn bạn, Cảm ơn bạn."*

Since my arms are in a hugging position, I lower them to Thang's height and aim toward him. But he backed up a few steps and offered his hand. Apparently too grown up now for hugs, but his smile revealed a full set of teeth, his baby tooth gap having filled in.

Now Anh. I got down on one knee and she flung herself at me so hard I almost lost my balance. "You be a good girl, sweetheart. I'm really, really going to miss you."

She understood the word "good" and I felt her nod against my chest. I pulled her away a little; then, not knowing what else to do, I kissed her ear. Anh laughed and rubbed at it. That's enough for me. I got up and walked out of the yard without looking back.

I drove past the rest of the villa complex and headed for Le Hong Phong Street and the center of town. Behind the high school, two of my candy kids are swishing palm fronds around in a mud puddle. Maybe because I'm not in uniform, they wave the fronds at me and started chanting *"kẹo, kẹo, kẹo."* On a whim, I stopped at the store and bought two three-packs of candy, turned the Jeep around and headed back to the mud puddle, but the kids were gone.

I sat there all alone eating both candy packs and the squid.

While paying for the candy, I saw I had the equivalent of $23 American in MPC. I drove to Hoang Dieu Street, where Bi`nh usually parked with his horse and buggy. I pulled alongside, reached over and handed him the money and drove off, thinking that was all the goodbyes I could handle for one day.

That night the squad threw a beach party. I think Sgt. Stubin was the drunkest. He came up with the stupidest questions, presumably rhetorical, like, "What would the Vietnamese do if it snowed in Saigon?" or "If a local ate rabid dog, would he foam at the mouth?"

At that point I decided to go swimming. The waves at Long Beach always seemed perfect for body surfing, at which I'd become pretty good. Only, this night, while standing shin deep in the surf, something bit me on the bottom of my foot.

Just then Wheeler hollered, "Hey Shults, your Korean sidekick wants to talk to you, he's up on the road in his Jeep."

"Yeah," I say, "Why doesn't he come down?"

"Beats me...he's your friend."

Sergeant Kim, "Why you hop like bunny?"

"Something bit me."

"Why you not bite back?"

"Cute, what's up Sarge...wait, how'd you know I was here?"

"It your first day off, you always go Beachcomber or beach...then Mai's. I have gift because you go soon."

He hands me his canvas pouch with handcuffs inside. He knows I'll have to turn mine in when I leave.

"Thanks Kim, I really...uh...don't you have to turn yours in when you leave too?"

"It okay, I steal more."

He shifted into first and drove off.

Even I have enough class not to spend perhaps my last time with Mai while I'm wasted; so I waited until the next afternoon, so I'm sure she'll be alone. Only she's not...when she comes to the beads she's wearing her blue ao dai, my favorite, several of the fake pearl buttons are undone. She doesn't pull the beads to her throat this time. She took my hand and walked me several paces from the doorway.

Before I can say anything...

"You go America?"

"Uh...yes, how did you...how you know?"

"Thang and Anh, *ba ngoai*...grandmother, my mother sister."

That explained a lot. Like how the Nguyens knew which day was best for me to eat with them. And why they always waved to Mai. But mind blowing nonetheless, since Mai and her cousin, Thang and Anh's mother, were so different, *me and Timi*.

Then Mai Lynne, still holding my left hand in her right, puts her other hand to my chin and asked, "You no...um...extend?"

"I can't, Mai. I have...I have people expecting...needing me in America."

She used her hand on my chin to turn my cheek to her lips. Kissed me and then moved to my ear and whispered *"mon depute fou,"* walked to her doorway without looking back, all grace and legs. Then, just the diminishing tinkle of glass beads...*mon depute fou* (my crazy MP).

I drove to the plateau and parked below it, my new favorite spot to gather my composure. I sat there a long time thinking, finally deciding I needed to forget about this place...all memories, good and bad. Starting with ... I rummaged through my wallet. It took a while, but I found my expired hunting license and hunters safety card mandatory in New York State. I took the stone steps up to the plateau and tossed the two off the Navy boat side and watched them flutter down toward the receding tide. I'd seen enough death for one life time. (I have not shot at anything that breathes since.)

As I turned to start back down, I remembered something: I had two small green pieces of paper used as movie tickets from the only time I took Mai to the movie house in the center of town. They're stuffed in a picture sleeve behind my driver's license. I hid them when I went home to get married. Turning back toward the ocean, I started to reach for them, but stopped.

I got back into the Jeep, then got out again. I took the narrow path down to Mai's beach, retrieved the two pieces of paper, and half covered them in beach sand, just enough so the wind wouldn't blow them away, placing one on top of the other. *Let the rip tides take them out to sea.*

Chapter 35

WINDING DOWN

The only thing that could happen that day to cheer me up, did. As soon as I got back to the barracks, I'm told to report to Lieutenant Whitlese ASAP, *oh shit!*

But when I got to his office, he said, "What did you put on the top of your 'dream sheet'?"

"Presidio, sir."

He smiled and said, "Well you got it, you lucky son-of-a-bitch."

I started the last day of my three off, Monday the 13th, the way I started the last 87, filling in a number on my FIGMO chart. I noticed there were only 13 days left. The last one is March 26, Easter Sunday.

I spent the rest of the day spit shining my boots, cleaning my .45 and drawing FIGMOs for other guys, soon to be short timers.

On Tuesday the 14th I got up at 0600, and headed to the mess hall and then went back to my locker for the rest of my gear. It was at this point things really started to go wonky. As I started back down the stairs, Nate Shanker was on his way up.

I said, grinning, "Nobody from Callahan's squad is allowed up here." Then, "Wait...you've got an hour left of graves, what are you doing here?"

He said nothing at first but climbed a few more steps with this stupid grin spreading across his face. "You need to, 'get your shit and split'," and hands me my orders.

Then, "We're going home, Shultsy!"

He had already started back down the stairs. "We've got an hour to change out of fatigues and into dress greens, that's when our hop leaves for Tan Son Nhut."

I thought, *there's no time to turn in the gear I'm supposed to leave here.* I'm not even sure which gear it is.

As if he heard my thoughts, Sergeant Stubin shouted from the bottom of the stairs, "Leave your rifle and all ammo in your locker, your .45, night stick and cuffs on your bunk, stuff the other crap in your duffel bag and get your ass down here. You got a freaking plane to catch."

Another major FUBAR, not that I complained. But it's a total 180° change in mind set. I went from 30 minutes before starting my first day back on-shift and the talk at breakfast of a party for me and Nate next time we were both between shifts, to maybe being back with my family 10,000 miles away in Schenectady in as little as 24 hours.

I stuffed my duffel bag with everything but what Stubin said to leave behind. The last things in were the fatigues I was wearing. I thought that my wife or mom could wash and press my uniforms when I got home. The only thing left on hangers in my locker were my greens. I'm reminded I haven't worn them in a year...there're too big.

I closed my locker door for the last time, totally forgetting to grab my FIGMO chart. I looked around, everyone's gone. Already off to guard mount.

Two new guys in Callahan's squad I don't recognize drove us the short distance to the main runway. The radio squawked, and I heard, "Unit one, this is two, over."

The guy riding shotgun grabbed the mike out of its bracket, thumbed it, and replied, "Two, this is one, over."

I heard Butler's voice, "Tell Nate and Bob we wish them all the best back in the world, and tell Bob I dug that .45 slug out of the ceiling, drilled a hole in it and strung it on my dogtag chain. I'll always have it."

Nate looked at me, the guy keying the mike turned and looked at me and over the radio I heard Jimmy Wicks shout "Hey Shultsy, we'll always have Singapore!"

Chapter 36

WELCOME HOME?

Our hop to Tan Son Nhut was on a Caribou. This time I not only cinched my safety belt tight but grabbed my sling seat with both hands, suggesting to Nate that he do the same.

An Army bus waited for us on the tarmac. We went directly from the Caribou to the shuttle, less than 30 feet away. It's full of duffle bags and guys from all branches of the service.

In Saigon we pulled up to a huge canvas tarp with 50 guys standing in line under it with their duffle bags. Beyond it is a beautiful silver Pan American Airlines 707, metal steps up to the door behind the cockpit.

Some sergeant shouted, "You will all *walk* to the steps when the door opens."

I guess he thought we'd trip over each other to get out of Vietnam, if given a chance. As we felt the jet lift off the runway, some guys cheered. Most did not.

Eighteen hours and two sunrises later, as we circled San Francisco International I tried unsuccessfully to spot Presidio.

Both Nate and I had a couple hours before our separate flights home, so we decided to find a bar in town and have one last farewell drink, to make up for the party we didn't have leaving Vung Tau. But there was an MP at the exit whose job was to tell GIs returning from the war zone not to leave the airport because war protesters were hassling the guys in uniform.

We sat on a plastic bench and reminisced about our year; the year I said I was going to forget. We toasted to our time together with two little cartons of vending machine milk. We were so used to the taste of that recombined chalk, it tasted like pure cream.

My flight boarded first, so we stood up, and shook as only Vietnam veterans do, clutching forearms like Vikings, then grabbing thumbs, swiveling to a regular handshake, snagging four fingers then pounding fists, once on top and once on the bottom.

I said, "Take care Nate. It's been...."

"Strange?"

"Yeah."

I turned, walked a few steps and heard, "Bob?"

I stopped, turned back and Nate said, "Ground beef and wax paper does look like brains."

I couldn't sleep the six hours crossing the United States any more than I could the 18 hours across the Pacific. But on the Greyhound bus from New York City to Schenectady I was totally exhausted. I leaned my head against the March coolness of the bus window.

The screech of a seagull, a butchered horse hanging on a meat hook from a tree, but the horse is in black and white. Now a nine-year old girl is lying in the middle of Hoang Dieu Street, making a "snow angel" out of a pool of her own bodily fluids. Mai rides off without looking back, leaving a trail of blood behind her Vespa. Two headless Viet Cong...bloated sand crabs skittering out of their oozing necks, a rotting severed arm, with a plank tied to it, now the arm is at my shoulder shaking me.

A voice said, "You need to wake up, you're talking in your sleep and upsetting my wife."

I mumbled some kind of an apology and fell back asleep. The next time I jolted awake, the couple had changed seats.

In Schenectady, I realized that the bus station had been relocated. *Had I been gone that long?*

I hailed a cab and as his current fare got out of the front passenger seat carrying a small briefcase, I gave the driver my wife's address. As the cabbie tossed my duffle into the rear seat, I noticed the back of his T-shirt which read IT'S NOT OUR WAR. I looked down at my ribbons over my left breast pocket, which included the two indicating my service in Vietnam, and I wondered if the cab company knew he wore that shirt to work.

As I opened the passenger side door, he growled "back seat."

Now he was all bent out-of-shape because I didn't know the directions to the address I gave him. Wishing for my nightstick, I kept my mouth shut. After he miraculously found the place on his own, I paid him, including the tip he didn't deserve, because I asked him to wait while I made sure this was the correct location. As I knocked on the door, I heard the cab drive off, my duffle was lying on the grass.

No one came to the door, so I tried the knob and it opened. *Is this where I live or am I trespassing?* Just inside the door was a stand with a framed photo of my wife, holding a little smiling bundle named Robin. I smiled back at them and forgot about the cab driver.

Now what? The only stateside phone number I could remember was my sister Margie's. She answered immediately, like she was waiting for it to ring. I said, "Hi sis," in my best, *aren't you surprised I'm home early* voice.

"Bobby?"

"Yup," the same sharp, crisp, voice.

Margie said, "How'd you get home so soon? I just called the Red Cross this morning."

My stomach churned as I thought of the little smiling bundle in the photo.

"What is it?" I asked, my heart thumping. *I've never even held her.*

Now Marge is crying. "It's mom. She was in a real bad car accident yesterday. I don't think ... we're not sure ... she's going to make it."

Then, like she read my mind, "Your wife and baby are fine. I'm about to ride back to the hospital with Les. When we get there, I'll send Harold to get you."

I waited on the lawn until my brother-in-law arrived. The passenger side door opened, and my wife got out. We hugged, and then both of us squeezed into the front seat. She said that Robin was with her aunt.

On the way, they both told me what they knew about the accident. I guess they wanted to prepare me for the worst.

Some guy ran a stop sign and Bill hit him. Bill was gripping the wheel and he was okay; but, according to him, mom never saw the guy coming and was jammed under the dashboard and had to be pried out.

As we approached the open hospital room door Harold said, "Bob, she hasn't recognized anyone all night or all day today so...."

I walked through the door and saw that they hadn't cleaned up her face, probably because it wasn't a priority. There was clotted blood all over her forehead and in her hair.

My brother Eddy said, "She won't recognize you when she opens her..."

Mom opened her eyes and said, "Bobby!"

I moved to the side of the hospital bed and just nodded, because I was afraid to speak. I was afraid of the sound that might come out. I took her hand. Blood was still under her nails and ground into her knuckles. I opened my mouth twice, and nothing came out.

To my right was an open curtain, beyond it a little nook with a sink and commode. I stepped in there and drew the curtain behind me to muffle the sounds of my sobs...12 months without feeling any emotion at all. I let it all out behind that curtain.

Chapter 37

ACCLIMATION

Just under seven square miles in size, Fort Devens is 46 miles west of Boston, named after Civil War General Charles Devens, who was also Attorney General under President Rutherford B. Hays.

The site was the home of the 53rd Regiment Massachusetts Volunteer Infantry during the Civil War. During World Wars I and II it was a training center for the Army and a prisoner of war camp. In the '60s several reserve brigades were activated and sent to Vietnam from Fort Devens, setting the stage for the last time I would favor my .45 caliber automatic pistol over my night stick for self-defense.

Fort Devens is 170 miles from Schenectady. It took a good part of my 30-day leave to get a compassionate reassignment from my duty station at Presidio in San Francisco to this one, closer to mom. They offered me two choices, the recruitment center in Albany, or Devens. I was familiar with the MP duty at Albany and remembered it quite well! No, thank you! I chose Devens.

We cut it close. Three days before my leave was over we packed the 1960 Buick LeSabre Les gave us with the few possessions we owned. We hoped to find a furnished place off-post.

We stopped at the hospital to see mom, as I had done every day since I'd been back. She said, "Bobby, when did you get home?"

As I stood there holding mom's hand and worrying about her recovery anew, it occurred to me that the whole family completely forgot about Easter, now two weeks past. In the four weeks I'd been home I had thought about nothing but mom. Now it hit me, and it was almost overwhelming. I had a new wife, a new baby, a new duty station, and they're all in a totally different environment half a world away from the place where I'd been so totally involved. My wife is next to me in the Buick, holding the baby, talking, but my mind is across the Pacific, 10,000 miles away.

The major bright spot in all this was Robin. At four months, she was funny, smiled all the time, and rarely cried. Plus, we lucked out and right away we found a furnished duplex.

The MP unit in Fort Devens was the 624th. Like the 560th we never knew exactly what our responsibility would be for any given day until guard mount. One difference was that Devens, like most stateside posts, maintained a stockade for soldiers committing military offenses. Everything from AWOL to drug use. That would be an unfamiliar duty for me.

The MP billets consisted of four barracks in a row, then our HQ and the mess hall. Most of the temporary duty guys were put in the barracks furthest from headquarters and the real MPs, for good reason.

Because of the war, the 624th was so short of personnel that the post commander ordered other Devens' units to loan men to the MPs for temporary duty (TDY). They were used for guarding the stockade itself, not regular MP duties or detainee work assignment guard.

The problem was, the other units usually sent guys they were more than happy to get rid of, even if only temporarily (guys like Scarface from basic). Worse, they were issued shotguns to do their guard work. Four shotguns were rotated between four guys per shift and they were stored in their billet. Hence the last barracks in the row...away from us.

~~~~~~

I watched an officers' foursome teeing off at the post golf course, the butt of an Ithaca model 37, 12 gauge, 8-round pump action shotgun resting on my hip. My duty that day, as was the case many days at Devens, was to guard stockade detainee work crews.

There wasn't much golf playing in Vietnam but there was tennis.

The night I guarded that high-ranking officer gathering, before Rico the guard dog and the whistle-blowing MP, I stood at attention near the door of the building, when General Westmorland himself walked by.

I was supposed to be keeping my eyes front, but the large white sling on the General's arm and the bandaged wrist, caught my attention. When I looked up, he was stopped and looking right at me...*uh-oh*, but he smiled and said, "Do you play tennis, son?"

"No sir."

"Well, apparently I don't either, at least not very well," nodding toward the sling.

"No, sir...uh, yes, sir."

The General smiled but the full bird colonel behind him just glared.

~~~~~~

Snickering, off to my right. The two prisoners I was watching that day were dipping one of their white arm bands into the gas tank of the lawn mower they were using to mow the fairway aprons and inhaling the fumes. Unbelievable! These guys didn't need guarding with a shotgun; they needed to be given prophylactics and encouraged not to procreate. I sent them knee-deep into some water traps to collect golf balls that I then dropped off at the driving range.

Another day I was guarding some guys cleaning up an empty barracks when an Army chaplain burst in. "Two guys with white arm bands are running across the parking lot." My guys were right here, so they were some other MP's charges.

I asked the chaplain to stay by the door and watch my two while I checked it out.

By now, the two were running diagonally toward my building, intending to use it as a shield from the sight of their guard while they disappeared into the woods.

They saw an officer at the door and an MP armed with a shotgun exiting the doorway, so they changed directions and headed for a different part of the woods.

I figured that if they heard me jack a round into my 12 gauge, they would stop. I did a one-handed grip of the slide and held it, raised my arm quickly and slammed it down forcibly, knowing that it would sound louder than a two-handed insertion. They both stopped, due at least in part because the chaplain shouted, "Oh my Lord! You're not going to shoot'em are you?"

~~~~~~

Four months earlier, on mobile patrol cruising Tran Phu Street near the toe of the boot with one of Sergeant Stubin's FNGs, we parked the Jeep so we could check an area bar that curfew violators liked to frequent because of its isolated location.

As we approached the window, candlelight revealed two GIs sitting at the back bar and a kid telling them and the bartender something while pointing toward our window. The bartender nods toward the back and the GIs head for the rear door.

I know these alleys. One way was a dead end and the other dumped out at Back Beach. I nudged my partner and he followed me to the open end.

I said, "Lean against the alley wall in the shadows. I'll stop them just as they start to run out." I figured that would leave them no place to go.

As I heard them approach my end, giggling like little kids because they just eluded two MPs, I'm about to step in front of them when both come tripping out of the alley and land flat on their faces.

My partner had stuck his foot out of the dark and tripped them both up. *I wish I'd thought of that.*

As they both rolled over, they're staring up at the two MPs they thought they'd eluded. I smiled pleasantly and said, "Good evening, gentlemen...how 'bout some IDs?"

Chapter 38

WHERE AM I?

Mid-June in 1967 the Israeli six-day war just ended but my domestic struggles were just beginning. I'm sure my better half felt that her other half was never there...physically or emotionally. If I wasn't off on some weird work shift, my mind was a long-way off. I suppose I should have, but I never told her about not being able to get that year out of my head.

I need to forget about this place...all memories ... good and bad ... and ... if I make it back, I'm going to live my life to its fullest.

I wasn't succeeding at either.

I felt that having a wife and baby certainly put a damper on *living life to its fullest.* And I realized that the memories would never go away. Part of me wanted to forget, part of me didn't, and none of me could.

My wife may also have felt that I married her out of obligation or simply to get out of Vietnam for 30 days, rather than for love.

~~~~~~

"Mom, it doesn't matter if she loves me ... or ... me, her ... over."

Then, "Listen! I'd do anything to get out of this hellhole for a month, over."

All of that was a lie. How do you explain at a crowded, raucous USO phone bank, that in just 3½ months I'd grown up...a lot? Maybe a whole lot faster than a kid should.

Responsibility goes a long way toward making one mature. I felt responsible for my duties, my buddies and now, my pregnant girlfriend. *In my world, in the 1960s ... at least in up-state New York, if you got a girl pregnant, you married her.*

In my eyes, Robin was the adhesive holding the marriage together. Three months later, we almost lost her. We put Robin's crib over a floor vent in the hall outside the bedroom because it was the warmest spot during the cool Massachusetts nights.

In September, the Army moved us on-post to save paying our housing allowance. The first night in the new place we spent surrounded by cardboard boxes. The next morning, we stopped by the old place to see if we left anything behind.

We found furniture lying on the lawn, charred and wet. Inside, we immediately saw the cause. Something had gone wrong with the furnace and it spewed sparks or flames up the vent and ignited the wall and ceiling.

If Robin's crib had been there, it would have caught fire first, even before the adjacent wall...perhaps God hadn't given up on me ... yet.

Mid-September, six months after my abrupt departure from Vung Tau, while cleaning my shotgun I heard, "Lieutenant Diamond wants to see you. Something about a Red Cross telegram." Lt. Diamond was our company commander and if he chose to hand it to me personally, it did not bode well.

As I rushed toward HQ, my mind raced. *Mom was improving. I'd seen her just a week ago.* I saluted but snatched the telegram a little too abruptly from the lieutenant's hand. He didn't seem to notice. Also, there was no empathy in his eyes, so maybe he hadn't read it. I quickly unfolded it, and read:

Specialist Robert G. Shults (stop)
Mother was in a serious auto accident (stop)
Need you home from Vietnam right-a-way (stop)
The bottom line in red type: URGENT DELIVERY

Yet another FUBAR.

~~~~~~

One of our primary duties at Devens was Post mobile patrol. We used OD 1966 Chevy Bel Air 4-door sedans, 250 Turbo Thrift Six. They seemed fast to me, certainly faster than a Jeep.

There was nothing like the rush of getting an emergency call and whipping down the back roads of Fort Devens at 90 mph, spinning bubblegum light (single red dome on the roof), its beam dancing off the trees, that's the good kind of adrenaline.

~~~~~~

It was 1600 hours. I just finished a static post at the Vung Tau air base main gate and headed back to the villa. I rounded a corner and right away the not-so-good adrenaline kicked in. I saw a MP Jeep on its side in the middle of the road, a bleating goat limping to the ditch and then falling over, and Sergeant Hemple holding his left arm with his fatigue shirt torn at the shoulder. Other Jeeps had stopped, so I asked one of the drivers to bring Sarge to air base triage.

A crowd gathered as I triangulated the accident. I did that by pacing off the distance between two stationary objects and the overturned vehicle (in this case, a large Areca palm tree cluster and livestock shed). I did this so CID or other agencies could recreate the accident scene if needed.

I kept losing my count because several locals were yelling at me. I thought I recognized the old man standing the closest, close enough to hear what he said, and understand the first part, "Bạn mông Mỹ" ("you

American ass"), then a few more words: "giết chết động vật" ("bad," "kill" and "animals").

A little kid knelt by the dead goat and translated the rest, "Why you come our country? You treat us bad and kill our animals!"

That was November 1966. Aside from some heat-of-the-moment confrontations with bar owners, that was the first time I was aware that the Vietnamese questioned our presence, and found fault with our actions, justified or not. (Sergeant Hemple was speeding to an emergency call. He swerved to avoid the goat that bolted across the street from the livestock shed.) *Hearts and minds...I know, Butch...hearts and minds.*

I said nothing.

As I drove off, the old man straddled his bike adjusting the cloth strap on his, *non la...wait, half orange and half purple with yellow polka dots,* I recognized him. It was the elderly guy Wheeler tried to up-end by sticking his nightstick into the guy's bicycle spokes. No bewildered looks this time...more like hatred.

Chapter 39

WHAT A RIOT!

Mid-October 1967, the 624th was placed on full alert. Protesters planned an anti-war march on Washington, D.C., slated for the 21st. That meant that we were to be prepared to ship out to D.C. on a moment's notice by military transport planes (on C-130s, the thought of which brought back such fond memories).

At the last minute we stood down because it was handled by the 503rd Military Police Battalion out of Fort Bragg. They prevented 100,000 demonstrators, including hippies, black nationals, liberals, women's groups, professors and a growing number of disillusioned war veterans, from entering the Pentagon.

Their activities during that mission received kudos from civilian and military leaders for their restraint. The Vietnam veterans in the 624th had several animated discussions as to how we would have handled it.

Race riots in the summer of 1967 and then the war protests in D.C. and at the Pentagon, had city police departments all over the country on-edge. The constabulary in Worcester, Massachusetts, 30 minutes south of Fort Devens, asked the 624th to send some MPs to train them in riot control. Anyone sent would meet with 20 uniformed civilian cops at their city's high school gym. My squad leader, Sergeant Lenard, picked me and one other Spec 4.

Okay, this was really my thing. It was like Sergeant Byrd letting me put my whole platoon through its paces, marching them around the parade field at the Academy. I realized, after I'd come out of my shell in high school and after 1½ years as a military policeman, I really enjoyed being a *big frog in a little pond.*

People being required to pay attention to me and do what I said became something I relished, but tried not to abuse...unlike Wheeler in Vung Tau. Sergeant Lenard and the other Spec 4 saw how much I was into it. They just stood aside and let me do most of the training. Sarge seemed impressed.

On the ride back to the post I was higher than a kite. Leading 20 uniformed civilian police officers in cadence, marching at wedge formation with an alternating stomp step, brandishing a riot baton, was way cooler even than using the pivot on a nightstick holder!

I pulled another special assignment, escorting three detainees from our stockade to Fort Leavenworth, Kansas. They must have committed some serious crimes to be sent to a federal correctional facility halfway across the country, so we mentally prepared ourselves for some hard-core prisoner escorting. But they were just kids, like us. In fact, I felt bad about thinking we'd be handcuffing them or worse on a public airliner.

I learned that we couldn't use any kind of manacles because it would upset the other travelers. That was also the reason we needed to transport prisoners unarmed, not even nightsticks.

We took a civilian passenger bus the 31 miles from Kansas City Municipal Airport to Leavenworth. One smirking prisoner cracked, "I wonder if the jail at Fort Leavenworth is a regular stop?" But after we signed the three over to Leavenworth's custody, and the gate closed behind us, and then the gate in front opened, none of them were smirking.

After signing up for a $2 room at the local YMCA, I spent most of the night at the Blue Moon "Go-Go Bar" in KC.

~~~~~~

The Army's Thanksgiving meal was an improvement over the previous year's because we could invite dependents and, most notably, for the lack of tiny black insects in the dressing.

Between Thanksgiving and Christmas my wife and I moved back off-post because some officer wanted our place on-post. The furnished house we found was fine except it lacked a refrigerator. Since it was winter that was okay for a while because we could store perishables on the back stoop, until the local raccoons got wind of it and we had to move our perishables to the house of one of our cul-de-sac neighbors.

Whenever she could, my wife was working to help bring in a little more money. Nonetheless, twice I went to the post chaplain to secure canned goods for us and Robin. It ended up eventually costing me two promotions since I got on the bad side of First Sergeant Lindal for going over his head to Lieutenant Diamond and then the chaplain for the second request.

If I had been given those promotions, we would have had enough money to buy the food we needed and she wouldn't have had to work. Something I was quick to point out.

By then I was desperate for an end to something...anything. Although it certainly shouldn't have (I had a beautiful wife and incredible daughter), everything seemed pointless.

I needed the adrenaline rush of the war zone. Something would have to give.

Unbeknownst to my wife, I wrote to the 560th in Vung Tau and the current lieutenant for the platoon responded.

Apparently, one of my sergeants extended and gave me a glowing referral. The lieutenant said they were in serious need of (in his words) "exceptional and experienced MPs." He checked with the provost marshal and he would "guarantee a promotion," if I returned. (One of the two promotions I was denied.)

Still being a specialist fourth class after a year in Vietnam and almost a year stateside, I was too embarrassed to give my current rank in my letter. Nonetheless, he and the PM promised a promotion.

Out of all my personally perceived screw-ups, I must have done a few things right. I could have been a staff sergeant if it wasn't for the two denials. The lieutenant didn't say which sergeant spoke up for me.

In the end, I didn't take it, because of Robin. Sadly, in seven more months, Robin would be out of my life anyway.

Chapter 40

FROM BAD TO WORSE

After visiting our families at Christmas, it became clear our marriage wasn't working. I moved out of the house. My wife met a guy from Oklahoma who was getting out of the service shortly.

Jason Gibbons, one of our unmarried sergeants living off-post, let me move in with him. Interestingly, Jason had this thing for Claudine Longet. He constantly talked about the time he saw her in person, playing the guitar and singing, like it was a high point in his life. The irony lay in the fact that Claudine's and my paths would cross eight years later.

~~~~~~

February 1st was a Thursday, one day after Tet started, when we first heard the news. Much has been written about the Tet offensive, but burned into my mind was a color photo of an Army five-ton truck full of dead and wounded MPs from the 716th.

They were ambushed on their way to the Tan Son Nhut Airbase and nearby officer's quarters, which was under attack. Sixteen MPs died. Over two dozen military police, mostly from that unit, were killed and 44 wounded, in the defense of Saigon alone. They were part of an estimated 3,178 Americans killed over the entire offensive.

There is a chronological account of the 716th's participation during Tet in Jim Stewart's excellent book *The Angel From Vietnam,* which account Jim attributes to Michael A. Rovedo's *Tet Offensive of 1968.*

The 560th's nickname was "The Roadrunners," but their slogan was "first in Vietnam." My unit was stationed in Saigon before being replaced by the 716th. Decades later I realized it was the hand of God that kept me alive. But, for the time being, it all simply made me more determined to keep my promise of *living life to its fullest.*

I started hitting the local bars in town and dancing with any woman who didn't notice (or didn't care) about the tan line on my ring finger.

I was supposed to be drinking alcohol to stay and listen or dance to the live bands, but I didn't have the money. I would look for an abandoned glass with ice, rinse it out in the bathroom sink, being careful to retain the ice and fill it with tap water. If a waitress or bartender asked, I would claim it was gin.

~~~~~~

Mid-February, First Sergeant Lindal and I were standing in HQ when one of the TDY guys burst in. Out of breath, he managed to sputter something about a shooting. That got our attention because five minutes earlier we thought we'd heard a backfire.

Lindal, "Slow down. What the hell you talking about?"

The kid just bolted back out the door, so we followed. As we entered the last barracks, a guy was standing at the end of the row of bunks, waving his Ithaca pump action 12 gauge around, almost like he couldn't control it, others were backing away.

I reached for the shotgun, but sarge beat me to it, yanking it out of the kid's hand. That's when I got the pungent smell of nitroglycerin, sawdust and graphite swirling in the air - the smell of gunpowder. That's also when I saw the body lying on the barrack's floor, less than ten feet to my left.

I'd certainly seen death before, but never dying. His eyes were unblinking, but his lower lip, already turning purple, was twitching as were a couple of fingers on his left hand. He looked surprised. Oddly, I saw no blood.

The young girl on the beach was dying, but I didn't know it until she was dead.

The body I turned over on that same beach was dead and decaying but nothing that looked like blood.

The black and white guy, dead-no blood.

The cart driver was dead and there was blood everywhere; blood that I purposely got into my hair and on my cheek.

Did my dad watch his best friend die? Or did his best friend die instantly? That too, would have been a shotgun. They were rabbit hunting.

For one horrifying second, I was disappointed I saw no blood, because I wanted to feel it again...sticky between my fingers. *Were dad's hands bloodied?*

"Shults...Damnit...Shults!" This was Sarge. His voice sounded far off. "Make the call. Get a meat wag...get an ambulance over here."

I don't remember moving from that barracks to the phone at HQ. My head was swimming with images of the dead in Vung Tau mixing with images of the Adirondack Mountains and woods where I hunted with Ed Weld and where my dad hunted with his best friend.

Him and dad laughing and joking as they climbed that farmer's fence before the shotgun went off. Then it was dad driving an ambulance to a Paris hospital, wounded and dying soldiers crying out in pain, blood splattered floorboards.

When I reached HQ, the phone was ringing. It was the PMO asking about all the commotion at the MP barracks. I don't know how they knew but I just said, "Send an ambulance to our TDY barracks. Someone's been shot."

That night on the couch at Sergeant Gibbons' place, I couldn't sleep. I was at the same time surprised, humiliated and acutely embarrassed because Lindal had to tell me what to do. But mostly I was bewildered for what was going through my head at the scene and on the way to HQ.

In my dad and Uncle Les' war it was called shell shock. After my brothers Ernie and Georgie's war, it was combat fatigue. I didn't know what they called it now, but I couldn't possibly...no way. Aside from my little foray into the macabre with the dead cart driver, the deaths I'd witnessed didn't seem to faze me at the time. Besides, many GIs certainly saw and experienced a whole lot worse than me.

Yet maybe it was because, in my worst recurring dreams, I never expected to witness the results of a shooting death in Fort Devens. Possibly I had shed the veneer of callousness I wore in Vietnam.

It was just two kids screwing around, mishandling a shotgun...*just like dad and his friend,* but everything hit me like a ton of bricks.

As I laid awake on the couch, something else was there, lurking in the shadows in the back of my mind,... something I hadn't wanted to dwell on for the last 15 months...something I couldn't even tell Mai about. Now what scared me half to death was all crystal clear.

Billy Butler in the cleaning room at the villa never knew how close he came to having that .45 slug in his head, instead of hanging from his neck. It was only the speed at which I went through the firearms safety protocol that saved his life. I was so tired, frustrated and angry over everything that was happening since we'd gone to 12-hour shifts, and add some new guy telling me he could hear the sound of a round being chambered, when I couldn't, when I was sure I'd left the clip in my locker, I would have pointed that .45 caliber pistol at his head and pulled the trigger just to prove that a veteran of nine months in-country knew more about his handgun than some freaking new guy!

Crazily, just the thought of something that might have happened, no, would have happened, further exacerbated by my father killing his friend, and the accidental shooting in the TDY barracks, still makes my stomach churn to this day.

Maybe my whole attitude was wrong in Vietnam. Maybe I should have handled a lot of things differently, regardless of one of my former sergeants recently calling me exceptional. Maybe I should have gone back, to do it right.

I finally fell asleep that night, with my hands behind my head, staring at the ceiling, thinking of a leopard gecko, white stripe.

In the morning, Jason, getting off graves, shook me awake so I wouldn't be late for guard mount and told me that the kid died. Turned out they tried to get most of the 624th to give blood, but none could because they were not back from Vietnam long enough to be clear of malaria or sexually transmitted diseases.

At the court martial, it was revealed to be just as I figured. They were fooling around outside the barracks holding a loaded weapon and acting like irresponsible little kids, so they forgot to clear the weapon in the sandbag pit outside the door. Remembering inside, instead of returning to the pit and pumping out all eight rounds, pointing the barrel into the pit and clicking on the empty chamber, he chambered a round, his mind elsewhere, and pulled the trigger. Only, not into a sandbag pit, but his buddy's back. Which he filled with all nine double-aught buckshot pellets, gangster loads, a misnomer the MPs' used. His friend was so close, that his body spun around, and he landed on his back.

The shooter was busted from private first class to buck private and, since he lived off-post with his wife and baby, he was confined to his quarters except when on duty and he was returned to his own unit, where he wouldn't be handling any firearms.

Chapter 41

BACKSLIDING

The aftermath of all that was to further convince me to pursue my new life as a bachelor with reckless abandon...*live my life to its fullest.*

Enter Steve Rickman.

When HQ found out I was living off-post without my family, I was ordered to move into the MP barracks, since I wasn't a NCO.

Steve, a TDY guy, was delivering the list of stockade guard assignments to Sergeant Lenard in our barracks. Lenard was the 624th's senior squad leader. That day I laid some albums on my bunk, having just moved in: Cream, Grateful Dead, the Doors and a new group, Led Zeppelin.

Steve, "Solid sounds."

Not really knowing why, I had taken to Acid Rock. It was a far cry from the country music Jack Garchow used to sing back at the villa. I just said, "Yeah."

Looking around first, and seeing no one within hearing, Steve asked, "Do you...uh...do weed?"

Now who would ask a MP if he smoked grass?

~~~~~~

Early on in my tour, I brought a combat infantry guy into the Vung Tau MPO. I'd never seen a guy act quite so weird. I handcuffed him behind his back, nonetheless he thought everything was funny, even asked if we had any pizza.

Eventually, when he started talking about inhaling marijuana through the barrel of his rifle, enlightening sarge and I with the fact that it cooled the smoke down considerably, I was totally freaked. I not only backhanded him across the mouth, I said "I ought to beat you so bad with this nightstick, your dog will bleed!" Partly because I knew Sergeant Raymer would be impressed. But mostly because I was appalled! How could we win this war if our combat guys were *druggies*?

~~~~~~

I heard myself say "yes" to Steve.

Although his family did not live in the area, Steve was staying true to his wife. He didn't take to hitting the bars with me. What we did was take hits on joints, something of which he seemed to have in endless supply.

His stockade shifts matched my duty shifts. Whenever we were off, we would hop in his 1966 Dodge Charger and head to Auburn, five miles further than the 28 miles to Worchester, because we were so paranoid about being caught.

The first time we made the trip, we found a gravel road which led to a point overlooking this mellow, peaceful valley. We always returned to the same place because, much to our euphoric delight, we discovered a monument to Robert Goddard commemorating our point as the place he conducted his liquid fuel rocket tests in the 1920s.

We reasoned that if Goddard could *get high* there, so could we. An added bonus to our heady reasoning was that he attended Worcester Polytechnic Institute near where I taught 20 cops how to control rioting pot heads.

We dubbed our spot the *Blast Off Point.*

On the way back to Devens there was one of those types of places that dotted the New England landscape: a dairy farm that sold their own homemade ice cream out of a stand in front of their farm. Nothing satisfied weed munchies like a banana split...even better than pizza.

No one ever found out about our joyrides to Auburn, but several realized we had an endless supply of weed. It astounded me how many MPs were now doing drugs. Consequently, no one ratted on us, in fact they came to rely on us to resupply their stashes.

Steve and I started making trips to Boston every time we were off. This meant I could add drug dealing along with cheating bars out of drink profits and of course "fringe" pimping for Mai Lynne, to my list of nefarious crimes.

Some friends of Steve's lived in Boston. One of whom was AWOL, and they lived in an apartment right across the street from the police department which had a potted marijuana plant in their window, clearly visible from the apartment. We all thought it somehow ironic and therefore hilarious.

I thought the two of them were going to crap their pants, especially the AWOL, when Steve first introduced me as an MP; until he told them we were just looking for drugs to mule back to a whole company of MPs.

We never tried to make a profit off the other guys in the 624th. We sold it at cost. After all, we wanted to maintain our *esprit de corps*. Also, add dereliction of duty to my list of crimes for not detaining an AWOL.

After securing our stash (while we were still straight), we would spend the night at their place doing grass, speed and acid, usually all at the same time.

One morning after picking me up in his Charger to head for Boston, I noticed Steve's face was covered with tiny pieces of toilet paper.

Nodding toward his face I asked, "What's with all that?"

"I was so stoned from our trip to the "Point" yesterday, I was still high when I shaved this morning and cut the crap out of my face."

~~~~~~

In Vietnam, I always started my three days off by stopping at a combination barbershop and "massage parlor" in the town center. The barber was up front, and the girls were in the back, if one desired more intimate contact.

I had gone to this guy for a real close straight razor shave every 12 days for six months. But this time he started to use a regular two-bladed razor on me.

I grabbed his wrist and asked, "What are you doing?"

He said, "American Marine say maybe I VC and try to cut throat."

I told him to go back to the straight razor. I figured that if he had wanted to slit my throat, he'd have done it by now. Also, slitting throats would have resulted in a serious decline in patrons.

~~~~~~

Thursday, April 4, 1968, around 9 pm, I staggered into the barracks after a trip to Auburn, just in time to see everyone either cleaning their M16s or stuffing duffle bags with gear.

Before I could ask what's going on, Sergeant Lenard said, "Prepare to 'get your shit and split.' We may be mobilized for riot control."

Two hours earlier, Memphis time, Dr. Martin Luther King was shot and killed. Things were already stirring in Trenton, New Jersey; but the worst riots were to be in Chicago, Baltimore and D.C. 34,000 National Guard and 22,000 federal troops were sent to aid local police.

However, once again we stood down. Still, it seemed that the whole world was falling apart, as well as my own little part of it. It was more bar hopping and trips to Auburn and Boston.

I'd been happier in Vietnam.

The only real diversion during this period, aside from the drugs, was hanging out in Boston Common listening to the war protesters and supporters argue as to whether we should have been in Vietnam at all. I always kept my mouth shut since I was usually high and didn't want to leave cloud nine.

Again, I'd been happier in Vietnam.

My life went on like this for four months. Then in August, my wife showed up at the MP barracks to tell me where she would be parking the LeSabre since she was leaving for Oklahoma with her boyfriend, and my daughter.

She was behind the wheel and I sat with my back against the armrest of the passenger side door. Symbolic, I guess, of the gap that had grown between us. Robin was with her and my little one took several steps toward me, her right hand sliding along the back of the seat for balance. She reached out with her left hand for me to take and pull her to my lap.

I did.

Then I squeezed her a few times and once again, not knowing what else to do, I kissed a little girl's ear. But before this one could react, I stood her back on the seat facing her mother, got out, closed the door, and walked away. She was 19 months old.

I walked around the MP complex for, I don't know how long, at least an hour, mostly remembering.

Robin sneaking up the stairs at the house on-post, standing at the top, her little arms flailing like she was about to fall. I would run up to her, my heart in my throat, but just as I reached for her, she would plop down on her butt and laugh at me.

Robin in her highchair sticking her neck out and popping her mouth open like a little bird, waiting for her next spoonful of baby food.

Robin in the same highchair, her face turning red as she pooped her diaper and then laughing about it.

Robin crawling around on the kitchen floor, opening the cabinet door and dumping cereal all over the place, followed by what sounded like "uh-oh!"

It's strange how you don't miss someone nearly as much as when you don't have them anymore.

Soon after my wife and daughter were totally out of my life, I ran a stop sign on post and was hit by some jerk, also in his personal vehicle.

I was the jerk for ignoring the stop sign, but his mistake came the next day when he showed up at the PMO and said in front of Sergeant Lenard and half the squad, "Since you ran the stop sign, I can have that stripe." He snapped at my rank patch with his thumb and forefinger.

This little puke, a private who obviously never went to Vietnam, and probably didn't even know where it was, was threatening to have me busted.

I lost it.

He was only about 5'7", but nonetheless I grabbed him by his fatigue shirt collar and shoved him against the wall...hard.

"You little punk, who the hell do you think you are? You threaten me again I'll...I should rip off your head and shit down your neck." *Sergeant*

Raymer. That's when I realized I was still banging his head against the wall.

Lenard yelled, "Shults! Shults!" as two other MPs pulled me away from the guy and I shoved my friends' hands off me. I saw sarge walking toward the arms' room.

"Get in here!" Then, "For God's sake, what is wrong with you? It's like you've been out of it for months."

No more than half the platoon.

"You haven't gone home to see your mom in weeks, but you're always off to Boston! Why did you turn down Presidio for this hole if you're ignoring your folks? You'd better straighten up and fly right ASAP or it'll be me that busts your ass."

I didn't know what to say. In the movies if someone gets crazy, a drink is thrown in their face, they're slapped, or both. It worked.

"I'm sorry, Sarge." I said. "It won't happen again."

Chapter 42

REBUILDING

It didn't. Steve was back in his own unit and I traded Boston for Schenectady. There was no plateau to park below, or ocean to stare at, but once again I did some serious soul searching.

I wanted to get my act back together. I'd done it before. I could do it again.

In Vietnam, aside from the cleaning room pistol discharge, my mistakes were small, anyone could make them. What did one of my sergeants say? I was exceptional?

I wanted that back again, so I went after it. Well, except for two things:

- I had the Buick towed to a civilian garage to have the right front fender pulled away from the tire. Since I was no better at auto mechanics now than I was in Vietnam, and the car needed a lot of other work, and I was short on money, I never picked it up. I rationalized that he could sell it for a lot more than the cost of the tow job, fender and the rest.

- The second was fun with Steve. Now, whenever I saw him with someone else in his Dodge, knowing that they would be carrying an ounce or two, I would do a quick whoop, whoop on my siren and switch on the bubble gum light. When he pulled over I'd walk up to his window in full MP kit, all serious. Both of us enjoying the horrified look on his passenger's face, and I'd say something like, "Hey Steve, you got an extra roach clip? I seem to have lost mine."

Occasionally I was assigned to school crossing guard duty. I know it sounds dorky, but I loved it. It meant standing on half of an inverted 55-gallon drum in the middle of a busy intersection in front of the school when the kids got out, in full MP kit including gloves and saucer cap, both white. Unlike civilian cops who always looked bored, an MP on traffic control meant specific coordinated orderly moves, heels and toes together, except when making one-quarter turns. Your arm motions said everything. Nice crisp salutes to officers. It was the *big frog in the little pond* thing. I was so good at it NCOs complimented the Provost Marshal on his choice of guards, which always made its way back to Sergeant Lenard.

~~~~~~

A young school-age girl in Vung Tau, about 12, liked hanging around MPs. She was one of the street kids that I'm sure didn't go to school and didn't look Asian at all, long blonde hair, blue eyes, and pretty as a picture. My guess is that her father was French and her mother Eurasian.

She also had a mouth on her like a longshoreman. She made us all laugh out of the sheer incongruity.

"Lazy-ass MP, you got sore feet? Get your own stupid squid shit."

"Dumb Marines...pay girl 15 dollar for short time."

"If I were taller, I'd kick your ass."

We all loved her.

~~~~~~

Having our own mess hall and mess sergeant, meant we weren't concerned about some irate traffic citation recipient cutting off our source of sandwiches for graves. Consequently, the whole 18 months I was at Devens, I wrote lots of speeding tickets.

The reason, for starters, it seemed that most guys who decided to re-enlist, spent their re-up bonus on hot cars. Needing someplace to really open'em up they figured there was less chance of getting busted on-post than in town...wrong!

If someone chose to speed, most likely they'd commit other moving violations as well. I would follow at a distance, so they wouldn't spot the MP cruiser, and let the violations pile on. Then I'd write them up for one or more, depending on their attitude.

A week before my entire three-year enlistment was up and I'd be heading home, I pulled a second lieutenant over just as he was about to leave through the main gate.

"Sir, you were going 15 miles an hour over the posted limit," I said, putting pen to paper and writing.

"I'm in a hurry and see this?" pointing to his rank insignia.

I said, "You also rolled through that stop sign two miles back, sir." Flipping the page and writing a few more things down.

"I don't think so...fella."

Fella?

"And you didn't signal your lane changes," another page, more writing.

That's when he shut up.

Near the end of swings, he walked into the PMO right up to Lenard, pointed at me and said, "That guy was disrespecting me as an officer!"

Sergeant Lenard shook his head and said, "Begging your pardon, sir, but that's not likely. Specialist Shults served a year in Vietnam and is an exceptional MP who knows both his military protocol and his duty."

Quick glance at me and (I like to think) the tinniest of smiles. Wow! I guess I redeemed myself and there was that word again.

Boys who grow up with fathers who were positive role models or authority figures that occasionally patted them on the back for even little things they'd done right, will never appreciate the feeling those of us who didn't would get, out of a compliment from someone he respected.

I grinned all the way back to the barracks. I took the long way, just thinking about my three years in the service. I screwed up several times. Knowingly entered into some of them, but overall, with sarge's words still in my head, I thought maybe I was an exceptional MP in the long run. I was going to leave the military with the definite feeling that I had done my duty.

It is indeed an extraordinary feeling to be appreciated.

Chapter 43

SQUARED AWAY

With only four days left in the United States Army, two more events attempted to bring down my positive exit attitude, but fortunately they failed.

Wednesday, October 16, 1968, about 1815 hours with 45-minutes left of swing shift on my last day as an on-duty MP. I was on mobile patrol and thinking about the next day mustering out and leaving on the morning of the 18th. I'd be leaving Devens, and the Army, for good.

Static from my radio and then, "Unit three, this is station one, over."

"Station one, this is three, over."

"Three, this is one. Something going on in the reserve area. Check it out, over."

"One, this is three, request more info, over."

"Three, this is one. A reserve unit has been activated for Vietnam duty and they're causing a problem, over."

"One, this is three. Roger that, over."

"Three, this is one, over and out." Whoever initiated a radio call ended it.

I wasn't far away, so I rolled into the reserve compound silent (no light or siren). To my left were 10 guys in fatigues burning paperwork of some kind in a 55-gallon drum and they're shouting, "Hell no, we won't go." An irritating hippy chant I'd heard often on Boston Common. Some ripped off their reserve unit patches and tossed them into the fire.

This really ticked me off. They joined the reserves to get financial aid for their education, knowing there was a chance they could be activated, but freaked out when they were.

To my right were about 15 more, half of them were trying to roll one of their unit Jeeps. Also, I could now see their reserve unit patches, they're from my area of upstate New York.

Now I'm ticked off enough that the adrenaline kicks in so my hands, as usual, start to shake.

I flicked on my bubblegum light and popped my siren twice. Admittedly, their reaction surprised me.

Somebody said, "It's only one MP" *(where have I heard that before?)*. Then both groups start for my cruiser, and me.

Praying they didn't notice my shaking hands, I made a show of drawing my .45, holding it in front of my face for everyone to see, jerking in a round and they all stopped.

While they're standing around discussing what to do next, I grabbed my mike and totally ignoring radio protocol said, "What the hell are you doing? Thirty minutes left in the MPs and you're trying to get me killed?"

A pause, then a chuckle from Sergeant Lenard, (apparently, I could break radio protocol on my last day in the Army) but when I didn't chuckle back, he realized that I wasn't kidding.

I quickly explained my status, then heard, "Three, this is one. Back away. Let the other three units handle it, I'm sending in the Calvary, over."

"One, this is three...roger that, over and out."

Before I'd backed away 50 yards, all three cruisers were either there or close, lights dancing off trees and buildings, with sirens, the works...way cool!

I waited until I was sure they could get things under control.

They did. Three MPs versus 25 rioters. I was going to miss the military police.

Chapter 44

"Shaved-Tail Looie"

All the next day while packing my personal items, including Sergeant Kim's handcuffs, turning in my weapons, and getting my exit physical, I thought about tomorrow and heading home. One of the cooks lived in Troy and had a three-day pass, so he said he could bring me that far and I'd take a cab from there.

Finally, my physical, and then a staff sergeant gathered up my stack of paperwork, my life for the last three years, pointed to some bored-looking officer and said, "The lieutenant there will give you your DD (Department of Defense) 214."

My DD214 is the last three years of my life on a single sheet of paper. As I walked toward the second lieutenant, he looked up at me, then down at the form. He did a double take back to the form and suddenly he didn't look bored anymore.

He said, real smug like, "You do realize you are not leaving tomorrow?"

"I'm sorry, sir, what?"

"You cannot leave tomorrow. You will be staying here another day"

Doesn't this guy ever use contractions?

He gently placed the form on his desk, like it's the original Magna Carta, splayed his fingers out and slowly twisted it towards me. Using his index finger, he tapped at the bottom third. Smirking broadly, he said, "Right here, Section 26a under non-pay periods, slash lost time," he actually said "*slash*," "It reads, '24-24 July 1966, total 1 day.'"

Again, I said, "I'm sorry sir ... I don't ...."

"You were AWOL a day," he said, leaning back, all smug again, like he just caught John Dillinger.

Then it hit me. That was when I was flying back from getting married and I laid over in Fort Wayne. I looked at him again to make sure it wasn't the lieutenant I nailed with three moving violations the week before and said, "Yes, sir. But I called sarge...uh...Master Sergeant Greene and told him there was engine trouble and I would be a day late." I tried to remember if Greene had anything against me.

The lieutenant leaned forward again, like he wanted to be close enough to really savor it, and said, "DD214s do not lie. You are staying here one more day."

He flicked the form toward me and said, "Dismissed."

I was not going to miss second lieutenants.

Okay.

First, I found the cook and told him not to wait for me in the morning.

Then I went to Sergeant Lenard and told him I would need my bunk for two more nights, not one. When I explained it, he grinned and said "I bet yuh I know what happened."

"You do ... what?"

"Remember a little thing called the International Date Line?" He's still grinning.

"Um."

Then he said, "You were having so much fun 'back in the world,' you forgot all about it, didn't you?" Adding, "The day you called in with all your MP Academy good intentions, you were already a day AWOL!"

In 15 months, no one ever told me this. It took that anal retentive second looie. FUBAR!

Now sarge said, "More bad news. Your replacement is already here. He's staying in our TDY barracks tonight, but I gave him my word he'd have your bunk tomorrow. He wants to get out of there ASAP."

"I can understand that," I said, without smiling.

Then he said, "I tell you what, Bob," *Bob, I like that,* "I'll call Post HQ and secure an NCO room in one of their barracks until you figure out a way home."

"Thanks, sarge...I really appreciate..."

Reverting to sergeant speak he said, "Now put your ass in gear and get your shit out of my barracks."

That night I stayed at Post HQ. The next day I spent most of my time in my room, because I thought that if some vengeful sergeant from headquarters realized an MP was hanging around with nothing to do, he would find something. Over the last year and a half, I'd written up a lot of NCOs.

As I lay in bed on my last night, it was a real bed, not a bunk. I thought about the first and only other time I was ever in NCOs' quarters, when Sergeant Byrd let me shake off my *Dear John* letter, so long ago, so much water under the bridge.

I went from single to married to single again. Crossed paths with several women: before, during and after my marriage; prostitutes, bar girls, Vietnamese girls on holiday, girls in bars near military bases in the States, Fort Leavenworth and Fort Devens. British Army nurses and wet coeds in Singapore.

I'd been bloodied by everything from a piece of flying Formica to other people's blood, lots of it, I scraped it out of my ammo clip, and my hair. Rotting flesh slithered down my hand. I rolled around in the dirt helping to handcuff alcohol-addled soldiers. I was brought to my knees with a mule kick to the groin. A chair was broken over my back (fortunately it was cheap bamboo and shattered like a movie prop).

Then there was Mai Lynne. Like I said, the most unusual relationship I'd ever had with the opposite sex.

I finally went to sleep, but not before deciding two things: I would try and keep the past in perspective and I would live life to its fullest. I would start both by leaving Fort Devens in the morning. Even if I hitchhiked.

As if the good Lord liked my decisions, former roommate Sergeant Gibbons happened to be at Post HQ when I checked out of their barracks, and he drove me to the west gate. As I shook his hand and wished him another encounter with Ms. Longet, I stood there in my khaki uniform with my duffle bag over my shoulder and I heard:

"Hey Robert, what are you doing? Going AWOL?" It's the couple from the cul-de-sac that let my wife and I store our food in their fridge last winter.

I said "Hey, Sidney. I'm going AWOL for good. I'm done. My three years are *đã kết thúc.*" Sid had been in Vietnam.

"Well, we're finished too, sort of. Thirty days leave back to Pennsylvania. You're from upstate New York, right? Want a ride?"

They brought me right to mom and Bill's front door.

PART TWO
CIVILIAN LIFE

Chapter 45

CIVILIAN

My brother Les and his wife broke up and he was living above mom's, so I stayed with him until I found a place of my own close to the folks. Eventually I found an apartment right across the street.

With Les' help, I soon landed a job with Niagara Mohawk Power Company, which was almost impossible but for one piece of incredible irony, four power company employees were army reservists in the unit I pulled my .45 and chambered a round on my last 30 minutes as a MP. I got one of their slots!

Despite the 8-year age difference, Les and I became remarkably close over the next few years. We learned to ski and joined a ski club. Les bought a small cabin cruiser and put it on Lake George. We named it the *Luv Two*. Those were heady times. We were like the prototype for the Festrunk Brothers, *"two wild and crazy guys."*

To get to Lake George and the Luv Two, I drove through Saratoga Springs, home of Skidmore College. On May 4, 1970, for a reason I was soon to discover, traffic through that city was bogged down. Just as it started to clear I saw an attractive young lady hitchhiking. She looked frazzled, but she was alone and so was I. Hoping she might like the idea of seeing Lake George from the deck of a cabin cruiser, I pulled over and she got in, but she was only going back to campus.

Before I could even start to convince her otherwise, she started pounding my dashboard with both of her fists.

"What?"

Now she's screaming, a high-pitched nothingness. The first thing I thought about, would she holler rape? She didn't know me that well.

Then she yelled, "I don't freaking believe they did that! ... how can they freaking ...?"

Again, from me, "What?"

"You don't know? Some Army guys shot and killed a bunch of students in Ohio, at...at Kent State! Just for ... just for protesting that freaking war!"

I swerved my car over to the curb, reached across her as she jerked back in the seat like I was indeed going to attack her and pushed the door open.

"Get out."

She said, "You're one of them, aren't you? A freaking baby killer!" as she got out of my car, slammed the door and spat on my windshield.

That went well.

~~~~~~

In 1972, the Lord took my mom home. At the funeral, Les spoke for all of us when he said, "There was never a stronger, more loving, caring woman than mom. She would do anything to protect and provide for her children."

Amen.

Having no further reason to stay in Schenectady, I moved to Lake George that year. Over the 1974-75 ski season our ski club went to Aspen, Colorado for a week.

We arrived at the Continental Inn on January 3. It was a Saturday. By Monday I was in love with Aspen. What ex-cop with an obsession for skiing wouldn't be?

Aspen is nestled in the heart of the Colorado Rockies, population 6,000, and was all partying and romance; romance in both its history and in its liaisons.

The ski conditions, from the knee-deep powder to the sunny well-groomed slopes, are every skier's fantasy.

But what really got my attention were the cops. They wore hiking boots, blue jeans, pale blue cowboy shirts with a dark blue yoke and police department patches on the sleeves. A leather belt on which hung their weaponry with any style of buckle as long as it was large. Blue jean jacket, also with patches. But the *pièce de résistance* was an indigo blue 4X Stetson cowboy hat.

You know my obsession with uniforms. Well this was the epitome of a non-uniform, uniform. I made up my mind, then and there, I was going to be an Aspen cop one day.

That spring I went back and applied to the Aspen Police Force, again staying at the Continental. The hotel owner was encouraging because he said that if I moved to town he would hire me as hotel security while I waited for a job with the police.

At the Cop Shop, as they called it, I interviewed with a sergeant and then took a polygraph, which as you might well imagine, made me a little apprehensive. I passed. My next interview was with the Chief of Police.

They didn't hire me because of my lack of civilian police academy training. But the biggest reason was because I didn't live in Colorado yet, and there were plenty of applicants who did.

All police departments have waiting lists. My plan was to qualify for a job in New York, thus proving another department was willing to hire me without civilian training. With that proof in hand, I would move to

Aspen and take the hotel security job that included a room which would meet the other criterion, being a citizen of Aspen. Like...that would be a real hardship!

That summer the ideal opportunity to prove my worth cropped up. The New York State Police were having open written testing and for those who passed, a full day of physical agility assessment.

I heard that 30,000 applicants took the written test and they were letting 3,000 continue with the agility phase. Due to my MP academy training and three years of practical application, I made the top 3,000.

What surprised me was that I passed the physical agility part. I've never considered myself physical or agile. My successes in the MPs were a result of my size, intimidating uniform and mastering the art of the bluff. Well, the pivoting nightstick holder didn't hurt.

Now I didn't have any excuse to procrastinate longer. The gypsy in my soul wasn't completely satisfied. Two weeks before Thanksgiving I started selling or giving away everything I accumulated over the last seven years. Early in the morning, December 1, I headed west to Colorado. I was 30.

I arrived December 3, very much aware that the day before had been my daughter's ninth birthday. The daughter I hadn't seen in 7 ½ years.

Chapter 46

LIVING THE DREAM

The best part about the Continental Inn job was watching the tourists. All excited as they arrived in Aspen and all bummed when they left, while I got to stay. I worked modified graves, 10 pm until 6 am. I would grab breakfast and be on one of the first chairlifts up the mountain, catching all that untracked powder.

My shift ended and I headed for the employee lockers and my gear, when this high roller Texan hailed me from across the hotel lobby, like I was a cab driver in Dallas. (My definition of a high roller is anyone who throws $100 bills around like confetti. There are a lot of them in Aspen.)

Texan, "Listen pardner, I bet my buddies I'd learn to ski before they got here. But it's been five days and I ain't done nothing but party."

I can understand that.

"I'll never hear the end of it if I don't learn. Do you ski? Of course you do, you live here."

"Uh ... yeah I do."

"Are you any good?"

"Well, I guess so ... not bad."

"Can you teach me something in an hour or so? There's a C note in it for you."

I was about to say, *"You do realize that's illegal... ski instructing for money and not being certified?"* But then again, he mentioned that hundred dollars.

"Let me get my skis."

~~~~~

By February, I was once again a cop. Which meant my skiing was free, as long as I took a list of ski serial numbers up to the top of 11,212-foot Aspen Mountain (locals called it Ajax, its' name during the silver mining days), and checked the racks outside the on-slope restaurants for stolen skis. Like with Nancy Sinatra, a dirty job but somebody had to do it. I skied over 40 days that first season.

At 30 years of age I was living the dream, literally. As a kid I always dreamed of being a cowboy. One could not get any closer than a law enforcement officer for a modern boomtown in the middle of Colorado, especially in that uniform.

"How do you spell that?" I asked, and quickly added, "I know who you are, of course, but I don't know how to spell your last name."

Talking to celebrities was already commonplace. They were everywhere, and I was a cop.

French accent; "L-o-n-g-e-t, Claudine."

"Well, I know that, I just didn't..."

"I know you know. I am just kidding you."

"Okay...um *Oui*." A shot in the dark but what did I have to lose?

"Oh, you speak French?"

"Not really," *she had the cutest smile*, "Well, a little."

"Say something in *Français*."

The only French I knew (besides-*mon cul*, preceded by the word kiss) was "*Mon député fou*."

She said "'My crazy MP.' Are you really crazy?"

I was getting there.

Changing the subject, I said, "Here's your registration card. Will you read the ID number back to me? I need to engrave it on your bike."

"Oh, of course. I would not want it stolen, would I?"

Then she may have said, "If it was, would you find it for me?" I'm not sure because I had turned on the engraver, but I like to think so. It would have killed Sergeant Jason Gibbons.

~~~~~~

As I said, celebrity encounters were common if you were a cop in Aspen.

- ♦ I helped Jill St. John find her dog.
- ♦ Jimmied Hugh Hefner's limo door because his chauffeur locked the keys inside.
- ♦ Jim McKay from ABC's Wide World of Sports asked me which mountain had the easiest runs, which seemed odd since he just finished anchoring the Winter Olympics in Austria. I would have thought he was a decent skier.
- ♦ Once, checking locked doors, I literally bumped into Art Garfunkel.

You didn't have to be a cop to meet celebrities. I'd ridden chairlifts with Linda Ronstadt, Clint Eastwood, Brenda Vaccaro and Michael Douglass.

I'd sat at bars talking to Jack Nicholson and Ed McMahon. Buddy Hackett walked into a bar that some friends and I were at and announced he would buy our drinks if none of us lit up a cigarette, and then he told jokes the rest of the evening like Arthur Godfrey in Vung Tau.

A date and I, and the lone bartender at the back bar of the Paragon, were the exclusive audience for an hour of entertainment from Wayland Flowers and his puppet Madame.

Chapter 47

THE SCANDAL

March 21, shortly after my snappy-patter with Ms. Longet, she shot and killed her lover, professional ski racer, Spider Sabich, at his home in Starwood.

Since I was a part of it, I've always tried to catch any media mention of the biggest scandal in skiing history. Everything I've seen or read has at least one or two things wrong.

It was the Pitkin County Sheriff department's bailiwick, but the police department always kept abreast of County cases.

I was an Aspen policeman, but I knew even more than most thanks to Roy Griffith who was to be my future boss. He was one of the first two people on the scene of the shooting. He filled in the blanks for me. Some of it few would ever know.

I won't point out errors in other versions, just relay everything, as it was told to me, and as I recall it.

In my mind I can still see them on the deck of Little Nell's at the base of Ajax Mountain. Claudine was on his lap and Spider was looking around to see how many of us noticed who he was with. It reminded me of a young sailor coming out of the Starlight bar with a beautiful Vietnamese girl on his arm.

That day at Little Nell's, someone said to me, "He's not always that proud of her. I've seen Claudine throw a glass at him for not giving her enough attention."

On Claudine's part, it may have been she who needed to pay more attention to Spider. Rumor was that he caught her in a dalliance with another local skier, a female. True or not, for some reason he wanted her out of his house.

~~~~~~

Roy's eyewitness account:

Claudine contacted the guard shack and told him to call the Sheriff because she shot Spider. A lieutenant with the County rushed up the hill to Starwood, running hot (lights and siren), stopping to pick up Roy.

When they arrived at the scene, they found Claudine squatting with her back to the bathroom wall, holding a .22 caliber reproduction WWII German Luger pistol in her hands between her knees staring at Spider sitting on the toilet and slumped forward. Roy said they assumed he was dead. (Possibly he held up his left arm to ward off the shot, which allowed the bullet to enter his side, puncturing vital organs.)

While the lieutenant talked to Longet, Roy went into the adjacent room. Noticing an open drawer on a cabinet, he walked over to it and looked in. He could see a small open book with handwritten text. As Roy put it, he used one finger to further open the drawer and read the words on the page. It read something to the effect, *He wants me to leave. Nobody tells me to get out. I'm going to shoot Spider.*

As the three left the scene, Roy whispered to the lieutenant, "You're going to need a search warrant. There's something in the top drawer of that cabinet you'll want." Roy then told him what it was.

At the Sheriff's office they secured a search warrant, showed it to Claudine and then retrieved the diary. Meanwhile they took blood and urine samples from her, which showed cocaine in her system.

The Sheriff, police department, and certainly Roy, thought it would be a slam dunk. A premeditated crime, gleaned from the contents of the diary, and its writer coked up to get the nerve to do it.

However, much to Roy's consternation, the DA could not use the diary because unbelievably, the Sheriff's department neglected to get a judge to sign the search warrant, and the blood and urine samples were inadmissible because they neglected to Mirandize Claudine before they extracted bodily fluids from her.

Claudine was convicted of reckless endangerment, a Class 3 misdemeanor, and sentenced to 30 days in the Pitkin County jail. She painted flowers on her cell wall and married her defense attorney.

My personal tie to the whole scandal happened just two days after the shooting. Local shops were already silk-screening T-shirts with images of Claudine blowing the smoke off the barrel of a pistol and the words "Spider's Black Widow." The media descended on Aspen in a feeding frenzy.

A reporter walked into the cop shop wearing a United Press International ID and said to the police chief that she would like to do an article entitled *A Day in the Life of an Aspen Police Officer.*

My chief said, "You do realize the Longet case is a County matter?"

"I do. I want to write a piece on the Aspen 'vibe.' What it's like to be a functioning part of it, and what makes it so unique. Who would know more about that than an Aspen police officer?"

I don't know if the chief heard me clear my throat or not. It didn't matter because I was the only cop in the place at the time.

He said, "Officer Shults...*Officer Shults? He never called any of us officers*...Take this young lady out on your rounds today. Show her our ski town and it's...uh, vibe." I stopped myself from pumping my fist and shouting "yes!" Big frog...little pond.

As we walked toward the new mall still under construction, the first thing she asked was, "So what's it like to be a police officer in one of the most famous ski towns in the world?"

"Well..."

Then she added "It must be great for your social life, what with a uniform that makes you look like the Marlboro Man?"

"Uh, thanks...I think."

Then I told her the usual litany of endorsements we gave any tourist who asked, knee deep champagne powder, 300 sunny days a year, world class restaurants and hotels, Aspen Music Festival, the playground of the rich and famous, and added, cops ski free.

Then another question I knew was inevitable, "Are drugs as prevalent in Aspen as we hear?"

I said, "Well, I've confiscated a few bags of marijuana."

She looked disappointed, so I told her the story. "I was in the restroom of a locals' hangout facing away from the door when two guys walked in and saw only another local wearing denim and a cowboy hat. They lit up a nice fat joint."

"I heard the striking of a match and caught the immediate odor of cannabis." (I used the official name because it sounded more cop-like.) "When I turned, I made sure my denim jacket was opened enough for them to see badge, handcuffs and my Smith and Wesson police revolver. I put my arm out, palm up, beckoning with my fingers." *(I didn't tell her that was my favorite "hand something over to me" gesture.)*

"They quickly gave me the lit joint, hoping I only wanted a toke." (Here I added "can you believe it?" for her benefit.) "But I told them to douse it in the sink and then give it over. That done, I used the same gesture with hand and fingers, this time they looked at each other and then both pulled baggies out of their pockets and handed them to me."

I guess she thought that story was cool because she never pressed me on the cocaine issue I was trying to avoid. Which was swell, since even the police admitted that, "In Aspen more 'snow' goes up people's noses than falls on the ski runs." Another saying used by locals when skiing, "Never leave a turn un-stoned."

She didn't even ask what happened with the two guys from the restroom. Also, good. I let them go. Otherwise it would have been awfully hypocritical, considering my own checkered past.

An hour into my patrol, a lady with her husband and two kids asked if she could take my picture.

"Sure, what do you want me to do?"

She said, "Just stand there and look gorgeous."

I glanced first toward the husband who was fussing with the kids and not listening, or pretending he wasn't, and then toward the UPI reporter who smirked and arched her eyebrow in an "I told you so" expression.

Turning back to the lady, I said, "It must be the Marlboro Man cowboy outfit, yuh think?"

After three hours of foot patrol and a lot of questions but absolutely nothing interesting happening (maybe she was hoping I'd foil an armed robbery), she said she had enough information for the article but still needed a photo of me "doing ... um ... something."

I said, "What do you want me to do? I'm sorry no one's been shot." I regretted that at once since someone had been shot.

Fortunately, she didn't pick up on that because she laughed and said, "Well, how about you write a parking ticket?"

"We have meter maids for that."

"Can't you pretend to write one?"

"We're on foot patrol. I don't have my moving violation tick...tell you what,"

I took out my pen and notebook, walked up to someone's brand new Lamborghini Countach LP400, all £120,000 of it, leaned over as if checking the license plate and put pen to paper pretending to write.

"How's this?"

She smiled, took the photo and said, "You do realize because I'm with United Press International, this will be in every major newspaper in America and Europe since he was an international ski racer and she is a French movie star?"

I said, "I wish I'd considered that, I would have looked at the camera, not the license plate." Again, she smiled, but didn't take another photo.

The caption read: "When it comes to parking tickets, Aspen Law enforcement officers don't discriminate between the rich and the rest of us."

Chapter 48

MY PAL, JOHN

John Denver owned part of the Timbermill bar and restaurant at the base of the mountain at Snowmass, down valley from Aspen. I became friends with the manager and would, sometimes, work security for him, usually on busy weekend nights when popular local groups like Twirp Anderson and the Hustlers were playing.

Security in this case was usually confiscating wineskins from people sipping out of them instead of drinking from the Timbermill bar.

An exception. One night a group of dentists were sitting together, when one of them decided a waitress's butt needed to be kissed...literally. Goaded into it by his liquored-up conventioneer cohorts, he crawled up behind her on his hands and knees and did the deed. Belle, the waitress, yelped, which got my attention.

I told the guy, now sitting on the floor and grinning, "Apologize and get out."

Which he did, but not before trying to collect several $10 bills from his buddies.

I said, "Hold it," took the money out of his hand and gave it to Belle. Not exactly a legally sound maneuver, but Belle and the other waitresses liked it.

He got off easy. My relief, who luckily for the dentist just happened to be a little late that night, was a uniformed Pitkin County deputy and Belle's boyfriend.

The Timbermill was also connected with concerts held in and around Snowmass. I worked them as well. I met Bonnie Raitt, Emmylou Harris and Jimmy Buffett.

I was asked to handle security for the Rocky Mountain Division of the National Ski Patrol's end-of-season bash at the Timbermill in April. They had a reputation as being a crazy bunch, but I didn't know just how crazy. *Maybe some of them were Australian!*

When I arrived that evening, they were taping black paper over the inside of all the windows. It turned out they were hosting a wet T-shirt contest, which was pretty euphemistic, since they rarely involved T-shirts or any shirts at all.

They also hired two bands for continuous music all night. And I do mean all night. I don't know what time the place closed, except that the sun was up. If that wasn't enough, one of the bands was Flash Cadillac and the Continental Kids.

The "contest" was to be judged by three celebrities, sitting just below the stage holding up cards numbered 0 to 9. The judges were to be an original member of the Tenth Mountain division, John Denver, and, I believe, Twirp Anderson.

By the time John arrived, everyone was wasted, so I was told to stick with him. After the manager introduced us, I sat with John at a small table.

Just 15 minutes and two drinks later, John asked, "Why aren't you drinking?"

"I'm security here tonight...apparently for you, remember?"

John said, "that's ridiculous" and waved over a waitress.

As fate would have it, the third judge never showed. After considerable waiting...and drinking, we all decided that the show must go on.

John said, "Since you're supposed to stick close, why don't you be the third judge?"

No objection here!

Three chairs were placed just below the stage and we were each given a set of numbered cards. The girls appeared on stage one at a time and beer was poured over their heads...pitchers of it, at least fulfilling the "wet" part of the contest name.

A dirty job, but somebody had to ... etc. etc.

Most of our scoring was based on the girl's raunchy dancing, more than anything else. Using that criterion, we held up everything from zeros to the nine and zero. Occasionally I would hold my zero next to John's, giving some deserving contestant 900 points.

Another time, the judge from the Tenth Mountain Division, taking his job more seriously than John and I, held up the 9, that being the actual maximum we were supposed to give. After the girl clapped her hands in delight, he took a second look at his card and said "oh, sorry," and spun it around, making it a six. John laughed so hard he fell backwards off his chair.

Chapter 49

THE VIBE

Here is my own take on, as the UPI lady put it, the "Aspen vibe." I once spent Spring Break in Daytona Beach, Florida when I was in my mid-twenties. A week of going crazy before returning to school for most, but back to the power company for me.

Except in Aspen, that week can be a whole ski season or even a few years. We were like Peter Pan in *"Never Never Land"* because we didn't want to grow up. We said, "When is the fun going to stop?" To the locals, the answer was NEVER, as far as we were concerned.

Here, the definition of "a local" is someone who has a mailbox at the post office and works in the support industry related to Aspen tourism: food service, lift operator, cab driver, cops, deputies, etc.

Our reason for living there was not our jobs. It was the actual *living* there that counted. It was a city of drugs, romance, music and phenomenal skiing, a lifestyle designed to help put off maturity for as long as you wished.

The summer of 1976 was one to remember. It was not only the bicentennial of the USA but the centennial of Colorado becoming a state, bringing even more entertainment to town than usual.

This was during the height of Willie Nelson's popularity. He was playing big venues like Red Rocks and McNichols Arena in Denver, yet he played Aspen in the Holiday Inn, not once, but *three* times that summer. He claimed he liked the intimate atmosphere and the enthusiasm of the locals.

His first time in Aspen he said, "As long as y'all want to keep listening, we'll keep playing." In an attempt to get us to leave, the Holiday Inn stopped serving drinks and when that failed, threatened to turn off the lights. They knew calling the authorities wouldn't help since most of the cops and deputies were in the audience.

Flash Cadillac and the Continental Kids returned that summer as well, playing in a small garden-level bistro in town. We packed in there like sardines. But the warm-up act was a comedian who just blew us away. No one had ever heard of this guy, but his lightning quick audience interaction, his impersonations, foreign accents and precise timing were unbelievable. By the time he finished, we all had tears in our eyes from laughing, and nobody really cared who the main act was. I didn't hear his name during the introduction, so I checked my cop's pass which read...*presenting the popular oldies rock group, Flash Cadillac and the Continental Kids, with their guest, comedian Robin Williams.*

Chapter 50

WAKING-UP

The summer was ending and so was my childhood dream. I had been hired at the APD with the stipulation that I would primarily be policing the downtown area and the new mall during its construction and I would be given regular shift work when a slot opened. By the end of the summer, the mall was near completion and no openings were available, so I was let go.

The restaurant, shop and bar owners, as well as the city contractor overseeing the mall project, liked me; so my termination was big news for a few days. Even the local radio station interviewed me.

That evening I answered my phone and a voice said, "This is Bob, right?"

"Yes, it is."

"Far out! I practically sang to that desk lady before she would give me your phone number. I didn't know they were that hardcore about giving out even former officer's numbers."

"John?"

"How would you feel about working for me? You've got more overall experience than the other guys. Maybe Roy would make you assistant chief of Starwood Security."

"Who's Roy?"

"He's the head of my security here. Tell you what, why don't you come up, meet him and then decide?"

Roy turned out to be every bit the former Colorado state trooper and as such he had been personal security for governor Stephen McNichols. Not just intimidating, but streetwise, intelligent, and full of great cop stories. Including the one about the Longet/Savage crime scene. It was like meeting the quintessential Old West lawman, I liked him at once.

Roy owned Doc Holliday's black powder revolver. To a history buff, being able to touch history like that, was really cool. As I recall, Roy gently removed it from my hand, laughing, because I didn't want to let go.

In Glenwood Springs, 42 miles down the Roaring Fork valley from Aspen, there is a bar and grill called "Doc Holliday's Saloon." Its' neon sign is a replica of a six shooter.

Roy said he'd try me for a month. If I worked out, I could be assistant head of security, which meant I set up the work schedule!

As long as I scheduled Roy for day shift with weekends off, I could work everyone else wherever I wanted. That way I was able to schedule my time, so I could spend seven days a week skiing. It would no longer be free, but a local's season pass, called a "host" pass, was cheap.

Laurie, a girl I dated back in New York, moved to Aspen in September. She lived with me over the 1976-77 ski season. I helped her get a job waitressing at the Timbermill. Unfortunately, that was the season of the "Great Colorado Snow Drought," so my season of spending many days on the slopes never happened and she quit her job because she didn't make any tips.

But that winter was not without its highlights. November 5 was the premier of the three night mini-series, *Aspen* starring Sam Elliott and Perry King. The plot was about someone suspected of murder in Aspen. What a concept!

We used it as an excuse to party three days in a row. We planned on having a different culinary theme each night complimented with an appropriate alcoholic beverage, Dos Equis with Mexican the first night. Chianti with Italian the second. Löwenbräu with German food the third.

We didn't know or care what the world thought of the series. We partied Aspen-style the first two nights and no one paid any attention to the TV. We lost track of the plot and cancelled the third night, German night, missing out on the bratwurst.

Near Christmas, Laurie and I, along with Roy and his wife, spent an evening at the Denvers' place with their adopted son Zackary on my lap and John playing his grandmother's guitar while he, Annie and the rest of us sang Christmas songs. The evening ended with John pulling me aside and giving me an exceptional bottle of Cabernet (which I kept unopened, for years - more about that later).

On New Year's Eve a few of the wealthier locals got together to rent the entire Aspen Health Club and Spa and invited all us *less well-to-do*. We were able to use the whole place, including pools, Jacuzzis, saunas, steam rooms, and ... private massage tables. That was the most decadent New Year's Eve of my life. Vastly different from the one I spent alone on a footlocker in Fort Gordon, Georgia.

Wintersköl is Aspen's annual celebration of winter in mid-January. Not having much winter to celebrate that year, we found other ways to amuse ourselves. Traditionally the Ski Patrol would make a serpentine descent down Ajax holding traffic flairs. It always drew tourists to the mountain's base and into bars like Little Nell's.

Since there was no snow, about 20 of us drove 4-wheel vehicles up Ajax as far as we could and then we hiked up even further. On a given signal, we all lit our flairs and ran down the mountain.

It wasn't exactly *serpentine* and some of us stumbled, nearly setting the slope on fire. We survivors regrouped at the top of the last ridge, lined up and flung ourselves headlong to the bottom and into Nell's. The bar went from being almost empty to suddenly packed. Thanks to the grateful management, no one holding a burnt-out traffic flare paid for a drink that night.

Later that winter, much to my ill-disguised chagrin, Laurie was hired as a deputy sheriff...all 5'4" 110 pounds of her and just in time for the County jail to host another guest...Theodore Robert Bundy. Not for long, because on June 7th he jumped out the second story window of the County courthouse and disappeared. For six days, neither Laurie nor I slept much.

I worked double shifts, my regular shift and then at night I drove around Starwood in my personal vehicle, shining my lights on the homes for the peace of mind of the residents.

I thought that if I recaptured Bundy breaking into homes or cars in Starwood, perhaps the "Aspen vibe" article and the outcry from my mall area supporters, would have the APD reconsider their decision.

Several times I tried to facilitate this by leaving my vehicle with the dome light on with the keys in the ignition. I crouched in the bushes nearby, figuring Bundy might be tempted to steal a readily-accessible vehicle. A little bit of a stretch, but worth a try.

The problem was that he was busy breaking into homes and cars on the other end of town.

More media gaffs. Some reported Bundy was captured by my former employer, the Aspen Police Department. It was two deputies. One of them, another female, told Laurie it could hardly be called a capture. Disoriented, hungry and in pain from the sprained ankle incurred from his second story leap, Bundy drove a stolen car up to their roadblock at the bottom of Independence Pass and simply rolled to a stop.

The media enjoyed a heyday, equating Bundy's escape with the whole town's attitude of lax morals, lax drug enforcement and now lack of ability to retain criminals.

That all stopped when six months later he escaped from the Glenwood Springs' jail.

He traveled to Florida and killed three more women, including 12-year old Kimberly Leach. Oddly, Glenwood Springs is the town another infamous killer died 90 years previously, almost to the month...John Henry Holliday.

The summer between Bundy's first and second escape, John and Annie brought home their second adopted child, little Anna Kate. My roommate and I decided to buy the Denvers a gift for her and one for Zachery as well, meeting them at the airport.

Since Laurie was a sheriff's deputy and I worked for John, we had access to a small part of the control tower where we were able to hear the communication between the tower and John flying his own jet.

Zachery was not with them, but we gave Annie both gifts at the airport. A few days later she stopped at the guard shack and gave me a thank you card.

Inside was a Polaroid of John with a kid on each knee. Zachery was waving and Anna Kate sleeping, both leaning against opposite sides of John's unshaved face and uncombed hair. He looked like he'd been up all night with the baby.

I gave out 8x10 black and white glossies at the guard shack with John's forged signature across the bottom (his secretary had it down pat) but my little Polaroid picture was one of a kind that I still treasure to this day.

On January 15, the month before Ted Bundy was recaptured in Florida, the Denver Broncos played their first Super Bowl. It was against the Dallas Cowboys. A big party was planned for game day, same as we did all through the playoffs, but a popular local's hangout, (the one in which I unexpectedly collected those two baggies of marijuana) had a better idea.

They offered 25% off all drinks if Denver was ahead at the end of the first quarter, 50% off if Denver led at half time, 75% if Denver led at the end of the third and free the rest of the night if Denver won. Only in Aspen could locals get a deal like that!

It seemed like every resident in town was there. But wouldn't you know it? The Broncos never led. Of course, that didn't stop us from drinking. By game's end, most of us were wasted and a little angry. Not because the Broncos lost, but because we paid for our own alcohol.

A guy I hung out with that night and I walked around town holding hands, hoping some Texan would mouth off on our inferred sexual preference, providing us with an excuse for mayhem.

It was spring now and I finally knew the answer to that question, "when does the fun stop?" It stops when you realize you can't live in Disneyland forever.

The ski season had been great. It was back to outrageous amounts of snow, but it seemed I had only three pastimes: working, skiing and drinking, with the latter gaining the ever-increasing priority.

With the ski season over, there were only two. I realized I was drinking too much when twice I asked buddies on the police force to help me find my car.

They didn't let me drive but just poured me out on the stoop of my apartment. I moved out of the place with Laurie. She started dating someone with the sheriff's department. But not before she smuggled two blankets out of the County jail and gave them to me, claiming they were used by Ted Bundy and Claudine Longet. How she knew that for sure, I don't know, but it was bizarre enough for me to keep both. I still have them.

Nonetheless, the fun stopped. It was time for me to leave.

Chapter 51

DENVER

A good friend from my Continental Inn days had moved to a singles apartment complex in Glendale, a suburb of Denver. She let me stay with her until another apartment was available. It was April 1978.

The minimum wage was $2.65, so I knew I'd have to work two jobs to approximate my pay with John and to survive in Denver. I looked for a job in security since I was too old for a new-hire police job.

Pinkerton was hiring people in preparation for the US Open golf tournament to be held that year at the Cherry Hills Country Club south of Denver, the same club President Dwight D. Eisenhower frequented. I asked for the graveyard shift, so I could search during the day for a second job.

I found it as a draftsman, something I did in my first position back at NMPC in New York. I was drafting during the day, on graves working security and between 4 and 6pm looked for a single job that would pay an adequate wage. Then I slept six hours. My social life was on hold.

Shortly after my birthday, I gave notice to my daytime boss, so I could use my days to find a job that paid the $5 per hour I needed to switch to just one job. Incredibly, he offered me the $5 per hour if I quit Pinkerton and stayed! I hadn't been so surprised since Mai Lynne returned the $8.

Andy North won the U.S. Open that spring and I started my social life anew.

Just before a Denver Broncos football game, at 2:00 p.m. on Sunday, October 1, 1978, in Glendale, Colorado, the most unusual relationship I have ever had with the opposite sex started. Yes, more unusual than the one 12 years earlier.

"Hey Gary, want to watch the Broncos at the Bull and Bush?" I shouted, knocking on his closed door.

"Yeah," he shouted from the other side, "I'll meet you there around 2."

Cracking his door open, I said, "Okay, but I'm leaving now. I want to see the start of the Kansas game at 1 and toss some darts until then."

I knew they'd switch the TVs over to the Broncos game at 2:20p or have a riot on their hands...Broncos fans are fanatics.

Gary was my neighbor and the Bull and Bush was a sports bar close to our apartments. As well as several TVs, the place featured a couple of dart boards. The place was packed when I got there at 12:45. Both dart lanes were occupied, and no tables were available.

There was one open stool at the end of the bar. I sat there and watched the guys playing darts across the room and thought about when I first got interested in the game back in Aspen.

~~~~~~

I was at the bar in a place called the Student Union. Three high roller Texans were also at the bar, very drunk and very loud. They were slapping down $100 bills and betting each other to see who could come closest to the bull's eye.

In darts, the foul line is 7'9¼" from the board. These Texans were at least 20' away and they were intimidating the other patrons with their bluster, not to mention risking everyone's lives and limbs by hurling darts across the room. People were starting to leave, especially the couples.

The owner tended bar that night and I'll bet he was wishing I was still a cop. I wasn't exactly sober, but the owner was a friend, so I supposed I should try and say or do something. Other problems: I wasn't in a uniform, had no authority and the only weapons in the room were six darts and three of them were in the hands of the Texans.

Tact was the only recourse.

I motioned to the owner to clandestinely remove the other set of bar darts from the display case. That done, I said, "Listen, gentlemen, we're having a dart tournament tonight and I really need to use that set of darts to practice...would you...uh, mind?"

They looked a little skeptical, so I added, "I'll show you how to score and the right distance to throw from, things like that, if you like."

They just looked at each other, shrugged and handed me the darts, flights (non-pointy ends) first. With that, they walked out the door. Everyone, including the owner, was surprised but no more so than me. Even more surprising, people applauded as soon as the door closed.

Chapter 52

SHERRY

The view of the board at the Bull and Bush blinked out for a few seconds as a young lady walked between me and the dart lanes. When she passed, my eyes were no longer on the dart board but on her, 5'6", short blonde hair flipped forward at the ends. When she sat at her table she was facing me, but she was looking at her girlfriend in the other chair. Now I saw full bangs almost to her wide set-eyes. She had a pixie grin, white teeth, great smile.

This girl, I wanted to meet! There were two empty chairs at their table. But I was going to have to move fast. If another guy saw her walk to her seat, those chairs wouldn't be empty for long.

Great idea...it could be my in. I walked over and said, "Hi, excuse me, but will anyone else be sitting here?" Mentally crossing my fingers.

One said "yes," the other "no."

The place was so loud, I didn't know who said what, so I pressed on, "I have a friend who is supposed to meet me here to watch the Broncos, but these seem to be the only two open seats together in the whole place, do you mind if we sit here...uh, for the game?"

They both shook their heads which could have meant, "No, we don't mind," or, "No, don't sit down." As a dart-playing buddy of mine would say, one always needs to try and have a positive mental attitude. He was referring to darts, but applying it now, I sat down. It was exactly 2 pm.

Positive mental attitude worked that time. Three and a half years later, Sherry and I were married on a small bridge crossing a little creek bisecting a park on the west side of Denver, in full view of the Colorado Rocky Mountains. Gary never showed up at the Bull and Bush that Sunday, so my wife still maintains it was all just a pick-up line.

We spent our honeymoon in California driving south down the coast highway. While in San Francisco, we drove through Presidio and I realized for the first time, what I missed out on being reassigned to Fort Devens.

We spent a night at a Huntington Beach motel. That evening we bought two beach chairs, a couple of blankets and two plastic wine glasses and then started a fire in a pit on the beach. We broke out the battery-operated cassette player we'd brought from home, popped in our song, filled the wine glasses with John and Annie Denver's Cabernet and toasted our future to Ann Murray's *May I Have This Dance* (for the rest of my life).

I was still with my drafting job when Sherry and I met. But sitting at a drawing board was not something I would be able to handle much longer. I needed to get out and move around. A year into our relationship, I started working for a laundry service. I was indeed getting out and moving around, but rolling up and carrying off dirty hallway runners, counting greasy shop rags and sweaty auto mechanics' uniforms was also not my thing.

Sherry to the rescue. Soon after we were married, she could tell I wasn't happy with my job, so one day she brought home a couple of pound bags of snack food from her legal assistant job.

Sherry, "This person comes around our office twice a month selling bags of food and everyone loves the service."

Then, "I bet you'd be good in sales." She should know, having grown up with a salesman father who sold everything from water softeners to silage conditioner to insurance and was outstanding at it.

I checked into it and discovered that these door-to-door retail snack food distributors were making more money than I was. That was the start of my own 30-year food business.

Four years later I sold my routes and we moved to upstate New York. I wanted to see if my business-to-business retail food concept would work there as well...it did.

~~~~~~

I knew my wife was raised in a Christian home but wasn't practicing any faith. Of course, if she had been, there wouldn't have been a second date, pick-up line or not. But one night she's sitting up in bed and when I asked her what she was doing, she said "praying."

What!? She never prayed!

You know my past, so you can well imagine my reaction. My feelings ran the gauntlet from bewilderment to frustration and finally a feeling of betrayal. Her faith dictates that Jesus Christ comes first in her life, even before a spouse.

Bible in my helmet liner notwithstanding I was still hanging in there with the mindset I'd had when circling Saigon so many years ago: if God did exist, I was sure my good outweighed my bad. Well, maybe at this point it was closer to a tie.

At any rate, I was not a happy camper. I even briefly considered splitting up, but our lives were so intertwined, and I was, after all, still in love. So, I tolerated her new-found faith, at times, just barely. Other times I'd go to church events. I attended her baptism but told her she couldn't pray around me.

Chapter 53

Blood Ties

We were living in Malta, just south of Saratoga Springs. It was a Friday night, October 12, 1990 and we were eating in one of our favorite restaurants

Watching a young couple at the table across from us holding a little girl about 19 months old, I mentioned to Sherry that Robin was that age when I last saw her. *When I stood her back down on the seat of the Buick and walked out of her life.*

That night, with Robin on my mind and feeling guilty that I never tried to find her, my thoughts were interrupted several times by my business phone ringing. I let it go to the answering machine, but the party kept clicking of, without leaving a message.

This happened three or four times, so I finally picked it up.

"Sugardaddy Enterprises."

I heard a woman's voice, "This is a long lost relative." Then she said the last thing in the world I would have expected.

"It's Robin."

I said stupidly, given the circumstances, "my Robin?"

"Yes."

"Uh ... where ... where are you?"

"I'm here ... well, Round Lake."

Three miles from my house.

I was so astounded that even the weird coincidence at the restaurant escaped me. She lived in Oklahoma but was visiting her mother, whom I assumed still lived in Oklahoma as well, rather than three miles from Sherry and me.

We made plans to meet the next morning. At 5'2" she was four inches taller than her mother but still a foot shorter than me. She had my nose, a fact she was quick to point out, but it looked a whole lot better on her. She was just as beautiful as I always imagined.

As my daughter, now 24, and I hugged for the first time in 22 years, I felt her stifle a sob as did I, but I could tell she wasn't a crier. She'd learned to hide her emotions over the years.

My ex-sister-in-law Janice engineered this reunion. I'd always liked her, a real sweetheart. She took that first photo, the one I look at as I write this.

Robin told me she met a guy while visiting, so she was going to move out here permanently. Just like that, I had my daughter back.

A few days later Sherry was waiting in the car while I ran into a little photo store to pick up some rolls of film I'd shot of Robin, when this attractive petite woman walked in to pick up photos of Robin as well.

What does one say to the woman who bore your only child and whom you have not seen for over two decades? At this point, I guess I could wax poetic and make up some profound, emotionally charged scene like a hokey B movie script - several pop into my head as I sit at this keyboard, - but I simply said, "Hi." Then I mumbled something about the only thing we still had in common, Robin, and walked out the door.

When I told Sherry what happened, she simply shrugged.

That's my girl.

~~~~~~

Robin and me. It never happened. Robin and me. War did strange things to my head, not the least of which was a sharply-honed sense of selfishness and irresponsibility. I was so determined to keep my promise of *living life to its fullest* if I survived the war, I not only didn't try to stop my ex from taking off with my daughter, I didn't even take time to find out where, exactly, in Oklahoma they were going.

In the 1960s women always seemed to win custody cases, so I used that as my excuse for not trying. The truth was that visitation rights would have been a hindrance to my lifestyle. But, now that I was married and settled down, I was ready to take my daughter back.

I've never said I wasn't pond scum...*fog of war.*

Well, not to worry, I got my just desserts. As much as I was eager to pick up where we left off, Robin was just as equally uneager. I soon realized her only motivation had been curiosity.

Although, during one unguarded moment, she told me that for a long time after she found out her father wasn't her mother's husband, she'd dreamt of me just showing up and becoming the real daddy she never had.

Instead she was left with the feeling that there was something wrong with her since her real dad didn't love her enough to show up? Though she would never admit it, that scar and its consequences will always be with her.

Whenever I think of my daughter, I am always reminded of a country song title: *Looking for Love* (in all the wrong places). Which in turn, is a painful reminder that she grew up just like me. Neither of us had a real father to love us so we both sought the love of strangers.

It didn't take long for Robin to break up with the guy she moved to New York for. She started hitting all the local bars with her cousins, still *Looking for Love* (in all the wrong places). *Like father, like daughter.*

A year or so later, she met and got engaged to Brian. That's when things really started falling apart with her and I. I assumed Robin's stepdad would give her away, it only seemed fair, and that might explain why I wasn't invited to the rehearsal.

Nevertheless, for days I practiced the toast I planned on making at the reception, speaking of some of my memories of Robin as a toddler, especially the one about scaring the heck out of me at the top of those stairs at Fort Devens. I wanted to make sure no one left that reception not knowing that the beautiful bride was my daughter.

One of Robin's favorite movies is *Once Around* starring Richard Dreyfuss. In the wedding reception scene, the father played by Danny Aiello, dances with his daughter, the bride, played by Holly Hunter and said "I've been waiting for this dance for over a quarter of a century." That line, in that context, seemed so amazingly apropos that I re-rented the VHS tape to make sure I got it exactly right.

That was indeed going to be the definitive father/daughter bonding moment, that dance with my little girl on the day of her wedding.

It was Robert Burns who said, "The best-laid plans of mice and men often go awry." It wasn't until the wedding, when I saw my ex-wife's sister's estranged husband walking Robin down the aisle that I realized I meant nothing to my daughter.

As if at the far end of a tunnel, I heard, "Who gives this woman to this man?"

"Her mother and me." *Her mother and me.*

The ex-sister-in-law, not Janice, without turning in her pew whispered, "Robin's stepdad couldn't make it."

Then she added, "She said you already gave her away once."

Touché.

The wedding party formed outside the church door which included my ex-wife and ex-sister-in-law's estranged husband, to accept congratulations. I knew nothing about him but from the moment he walked my daughter down the aisle, I hated him. Shaking his hand was not something I could handle...no way.

We went out a side door, headed straight home and stayed there. I think Sherry drove.

Chapter 54

HOME AND HORROR

It was now spring of 1994. I was Scoutmaster for a Troop in Alplaus for most of the six years we lived in New York. The troop went to the Boy Scout Jamboree in 1993, held every four years at Fort A. P. Hill, Virginia.

We also went to the West Point Military Academy Camporee twice, which was by invitation only, and the unit earned several other awards. During my tenure, seven scouts made Eagle.

However, Sherry and I were both homesick for Colorado. If things had worked out with Robin, you would have had to pry me out of New York with a crowbar. Before the wedding I imagined things like watching NFL games at my daughter and son-in-law's home with a grandchild or two on my lap. As it was, there was nothing to keep us in the east.

We put my route up for sale and moved back home to Colorado in October.

I got the business back up-to-speed and took up serious bicycling, which included charity, endurance and multi-day rides and, of course, we fell back in love with Colorado.

Tuesday, April 20, 1999, I had just left an office building and lifted my two-wheeled selling cart back into my van. I turned on the radio and started unwrapping my lunch. I liked eating at what I called *the dashboard diner*.

On the radio I heard a local news anchor, her voice breaking, "This was the last bus arriving at the elementary school from the scene of all this, this horror, and the mothers of the kids not on the bus were getting sick, even vomiting."

That's how I first heard about the Columbine High School killings in Littleton, less than 18 miles from where we lived in Aurora.

The whole world was glued to the newscasts all the rest of that week. On Saturday, Sherry and I drove to Littleton, stopping at a florist to buy flowers to lay at the makeshift memorial we'd watched grow over the last four days on the TV news.

Sherry, "We need 13 flowers."

"You're going to the high school, aren't you? People have been stopping here since Tuesday, buying the same amount."

There were so many cars we parked five blocks from the site. The memorial appeared to have started on the grass in front of 17-year old Rachel Scott's red 1988 Acura Legend which had been moved from the senior high school parking lot to a park near the school. She was the first to die.

Teenage girls were standing in groups, hugging and weeping. I'd seen that before. Not one of my favorite memories. I'd also seen makeshift memorials. I attended the one for the three MPs, Patrick Brems, his lieutenant and the lieutenant's driver, killed in the Victoria Hotel attack, but I'd never seen anything like this.

(At military memorials, it's tradition to thrust bayonet-mounted rifles into the ground, rest the steel helmets or, in the case of MPs, helmet liners of the fallen on the butts of the stock and set their boots on the ground by the rifle muzzle.)

This memorial near Columbine High School exhibited a macabre, yet strangely beautiful, symmetry. It seemed to grow from the grass in front of Rachel's car in both directions and in height to completely obscure the median. It had rained since the car was moved, and it was drizzling as we stood there, raindrops underscoring the somber mood as if everyone and everything was weeping.

People covered the first layer of mementos with sheets of clear plastic and a second row was growing on top of the first. A canopy had been erected over the car and the car was covered with plush animals, flowers, photos and poster-sized "letters" to Rachel.

The 2016 movie, *I'm Not Ashamed* about Rachel Joy Scott, is a powerful, moving story and a reminder that if we put our lives into God's hands, it can make an enormous difference. Something I was soon to learn.

~~~~~~

Then the event that changed our world: September 11, 2001. Like every horrific event this country has suffered, everyone remembers where they were and what they were doing when they heard.

For my part, I stopped loading my company van and drove to the nearest blood bank, and like many others, waited in line for hours, the neighboring businesses supplying everyone with water and snacks.

Chapter 55

EPIPHANY

Labor Day, Monday, September 3, seven days before the Twin Towers fell, and seven years after we moved back to Colorado, the most profoundly significant event in my life began to unfold.

I was straddling my bike in a little pull-off on US 34 as it rose above the mountain town of Estes Park. I was there because, in mid-August I entered the 100-mile Tour de Cure bicycle ride for the American Diabetes Association.

The most challenging part of that ride was the climb up "Devil's Gulch." The Gulch has a 15% grade and is about one mile in length with two switchbacks. To put this in perspective, most paved road bike climbs in the Colorado Rockies are 6½%, which is a challenge for many bicyclists. Devil's Gulch is more than twice that grade.

Riders actually keep track of how many times they've attempted Devil's Gulch and made it without stopping. My attempt for the Tour de Cure was my first and I did end up stopping to catch my breath, even though I was in my best cycling shape at the time.

I was irritated about failing in August, so I was back at it on Labor Day. This time I made it. The complete Devil's Gulch loop starts in the town of Drake on County Road 43, through Glen Haven to the top of the two switchbacks, then down into Estes Park past the Stanley Hotel (Stephen King's inspiration for his book *The Shining*), and then back to Drake via US 34

I stood there, feeling quite self-satisfied with my accomplishment when, for no apparent reason, my wife's faith came to mind. A faith that seemed to be growing exponentially and how my heart was now softening toward that same faith.

As I looked back toward Estes Park and the magnificent grandeur of the 13-14,000-foot-high snow-capped peaks that tower above the town, the two lakes and the Big Thomson River, Aspen trees just starting to take on their golden hue contrasted against the green of the Lodge pole pine, I heard the shrill whistle and shuddering bellow of a bull elk, which drew my eyes to a field of wild flowers by the lakes. Several cow elk and a huge bull were grazing in the field.

I heard the honking of several Canadian Geese overhead and my gaze turned skyward, when a Bible verse Sherry had been quoting recently, came to mind. Romans 1:20 *"For since the creation of the world His invisible attributes, His eternal power and divine nature, have been clearly seen, being understood through what has been made, so that they are without excuse."*

The last part of the verse, *"so that they are without excuse,"* got my attention the first time, even more so at that moment, as the sound of the geese faded, and I looked around me at all that glorious beauty.

Pastor teacher, John MacArthur's commentary on those last six words of Romans 1:20 reads:

> "God *holds* all men responsible for their refusal to acknowledge what he has shown them of himself in His creation, even those who have never had an opportunity to hear the gospel have received a clear witness about the existence and character of God-and have suppressed it. If a person will respond to the revelation he has, even if it is solely natural revelation, God will provide some means for that person to hear the gospel."

I don't even remember starting, but still looking heavenward, I heard myself praying out loud, the first time since I was a kid. "Lord, what do I do now? I don't know what to do. I need your help with all of this...any of this."

~~~~~~

September 15. I was in Leadville for the start of the 89-mile Biketoberfest ride for multiple scleroses. The route is also known as the Copper Triangle, involving four challenging climbs and grades averaging 6½%.

It was freezing that morning as we started our climb up Fremont Pass. The higher we climbed, the colder we got. In late August I was in Wichita Falls, Texas for the Hotter N Hell Hundred and I remembered that the headband I'd used to keep the sweat out of my eyes, was still stuffed in my bullet bag. I now used it to keep my ears warm.

By the time I reached the top of Fremont Pass, I was wearing every piece of clothing I brought and even my water bottle had a thin layer of ice.

Then incredibly, the clouds dispersed, the sun shone, birds chirped, and it warmed up considerably on the descent. It was going to be a beautiful day.

For once I was not thinking about God. Something I had done constantly since Estes Park. I was just thankful I survived Fremont Pass in one piece.

At the bottom lay Copper Mountain Ski Resort, just before Route 91 merges onto Interstate 70. I still vividly remember a Summit County deputy sheriff stopping traffic in both directions to allow us cyclists to turn left into the entrance of the Resort. Our next challenge was to be Vail Pass, starting at the west end of Copper Mountain.

However, just as I turned, my life, indeed my whole world, turned with me. I was looking at the ski slopes, now barren of snow, when I felt an incredible warmth. Not from the sun but growing from within me and spreading outward.

I felt like an unborn child must feel inside his mother's womb, warm, safe and extremely well-loved, incomprehensively so.

I felt, rather than heard, a voice saying, "It's time, Bob...it's time." I was filled with a sense of well-being that was overwhelming. I was consumed with total joy and wonder.

I gasped then tried not to sob, but failed. Then the tears came, and I wept freely. Without realizing it, I stopped riding and unclipped, straddling my bike as I did above Estes Park, bikes passing me in a blur because my eyes were full of tears.

There was a little pull-off across the entry road where a few riders were stopping to remove the clothing layers they no longer needed. I backhanded the tears off my face with my riding gloves as I walked by them, hands shaking in spite of my death grip on the handlebars.

I thought for sure they would see some kind of, I don't know, change in this person they chatted with all the way up Fremont Pass, mostly about how cold they were, some kind of glow ... something.

Those of you who know your Bible will recall the Apostle Paul's conversion on his way to Damascus. Well this was in no way even close to that, of course, but it was close enough for me and I'm a hard sell, *if there is a God, I'm sure my good outweighs my bad.*

Interestingly, I kept all this to myself, not even telling Sherry. I needed time to wrap my mind around it. I didn't think anyone other than my wife would believe me. Did I even believe it? Could I have imagined it? But if so, why?

On September 3, I asked the Lord for his help, 26 days later, He delivered...in spades. I call it my Copper Mountain epiphany.

Chapter 56

SHARING THE GOSPEL

On September 29, a cycling buddy asked if I wanted to join three others in a climb up Mount Evans (it's the highest paved road in North America). We started at Echo Lake, which was the site of the final scene in the cycling movie *American Flyer* starring Kevin Costner, and David Grant. Elevation 10,600 feet. The summit of Evans is over 14,200. The distance is nine miles, making it an elevation gain of 3,600 feet and an average incline of about 9% with one nasty section at 15%, just as you passed Summit Lake.

Having done this climb previously, my buddy wasn't going to ride this time, but he was going to film it Tour de France style from his vehicle, shooting alongside us as we rounded most of the 14 hairpin switchbacks.

After reaching the top and catching our breath, we started back down. Being the wuss I am when it comes to fast descents, I was soon left in the dust. Being alone gave me plenty of time to think, mostly about my Estes Park experience and the Copper Mountain epiphany.

Although somewhat distracted by the lack of any shoulders or guardrails on those 14 hairpin turns and their 800 to 900-foot drop offs, I decided, for sure, I was going to "accept Jesus."

The next weekend, Sherry's parents were coming to Denver from Nebraska and planned on going to Sherry's church. My attendance would not necessarily be a surprise but going up to the front of the church at altar call to accept Jesus would certainly be.

However, the next day at church, Pastor talked about heaven and I felt Sherry's grip tighten over my hand. I turned toward her to see eyes welling up with tears. After service, during lunch at a restaurant, I asked her why she was crying...although I knew. She said some day she would never see me again since I wasn't saved and, once more started crying. I couldn't handle any more tears, so I told her all about Estes Park and the Copper Mountain epiphany ending with my thought on surprising mom and dad with my "altar call salvation."

The first thing she said was "No!"

"No? What?"

"No, you can't wait till then. You need to do it now."

Of course, Sherry knew one does not have to have a pastor present to come to Christ, but she figured I would assume as much and she wasn't about to confuse the issue with facts.

So off we went, back to the church. My wife called the pastor on her cell while I drove. I'm not sure what she told him since her explanation as to why we'd like to see him back in his office was punctuated with admonitions toward me:

"Use your blinker!"

"Slow down, honey!"

"Watch that car on your right!"

Apparently. she was afraid I might die before I was to live eternally with the Lord.

I've got to hand it to Pastor Bob. Just an hour after leaving church, he returned on my account. This time in print shirt, cargo shorts and flip-flops. He asked me a couple of questions, suggested a few things I should say in prayer, which I did and that was it. We shook hands and decided I'd be baptized when mom and dad were here, and we left.

As soon as we got home, Sherry called her parents and all four siblings. That meant calls to South Dakota, Nebraska, Georgia and Spain where her brother Bob and his family were missionaries.

Chapter 57

DEATH AT MIDNIGHT

In July 2012, the annual Courage Classic Bicycle Tour for Children's Hospital took place on Saturday through Monday, July 21-23. I'd ridden it several times, so Sherry and I volunteered to work rest stops that year.

As we settled into our hotel room at Copper Mountain Friday afternoon, I turned on the TV and saw what looked like the gaudy neon facade of the Century 16 Theater less than 10 miles from our home in Aurora.

It couldn't be a live shot. It was night on the screen, alternating red and blue LED light bars of cop cars illuminating the parking lot surrounded with yellow police tape and we heard talk of yet another mass shooting.

Not again! As we sat on the edge of the bed watching in horror, we learned 12 people died and 70 were injured.

We prayed for those involved, never thinking we knew any of the victims. We stayed for the Tour and tended to our volunteer work.

We were wrong. We knew three of them, one of whom was seriously wounded.

Eugene is the eldest son of our best friends from Pastor Bob's church. I worked with him, KC and Luke in the high school age youth group. Adan and Jennifer joined their church after Sherry and I had moved on.

Now in their early twenties, three of the former high schoolers were in theater number nine of the Century 16 Cineplex for the midnight premier of *The Dark Knight Rises*.

~~~~~~

The five close friends ate at Village Inn around 7:30 Thursday evening, the 19th. Eugene and KC had been engaged since April; Jennifer and Adan were married less than a year. The fifth friend was Luke.

After dinner, the five of them went to Adan and Jennifer's place to await the start of the movie's midnight premier. Then, because they thought that the theater would be packed, they decided to get there an hour and a half early.

Even at 10:30, theater number 9 was almost full. The only place with five seats together was row 9, the first five off the aisle. Luke sat on the end, then Eugene, KC, Jennifer and Adan.

The movie started at five minutes after midnight. Thirty-three minutes later, a man dressed in riot gear, armed with a shotgun, .40 caliber pistol, two smoke canisters and an AR15, (very similar to the M16s we carried in Vietnam), entered the theater at the foot of the aisle where the five friends were sitting.

On the screen a shooting scene had just started when Eugene heard popping sounds and saw smoke from the canister that was thrown a few rows behind them to their left. He first thought that someone tossed firecrackers into one of the aisles. KC thought they were part of the movie.

Now the killer walked the wide aisle parallel to the screen, two rows in front of them, firing toward the back rows with the AR15 which he swept in an arc to his right, penetrating the wall separating screens nine and eight, wounding three people in the adjacent theater.

All five dove for the floor, Eugene pulled KC down with him, the guys attempted to shield the women. A round soon slammed into his fiancé's now-empty seat.

From the gap between the seats in front of him, Eugene could see the shooter moving up and down the aisle. Dressed entirely in black, wearing a gasmask, helmet, and flack vest and illuminated by the strobing lights from the movie filtered through smoke from the canisters. Now screams and cries of pain. Sights and sounds all coalesced into an apocalyptic nightmare.

Then he was shot.

In Eugene's words, "It felt like being hit by a fastball thrown by a professional pitcher."

Having been hit in the right hip, his leg jerked up reflexively and another round hit his knee.

"Then came the excruciating heat from the fragmented round in my hip."

After what seemed like an eternity, the shooting stopped [CSI and ATF eventually said that 65 rounds were fired from the rifle alone]. Eugene figured the shooter must be reloading [actually, his drum-style ammo feeder jammed].

Eugene, "We have to leave now!"

The closest exit was the door the killer had used to enter theater 9. Eugene realized that if he kept his knee locked, he could manage to stand on his right leg, that wound being through and through.

A wall separated their aisle from the ramp leading up from the main Cineplex lobby. Going down the stairs, Eugene tripped, and Luke helped him up.

As the five of them cleared the wall at the top of the ramp they saw the killer just a few feet down the incline, trying to un-jam his assault rifle. He looked up at them, and they looked down at him. KC made eye contact with the shooter and their eyes locked.

She said, "I felt like a deer in the headlights."

Somehow, they made it out the door. That's when Eugene realized Adan was shot as well. He was hit in the right shin, shattering both tibia and fibula. Luke switched from supporting Eugene to helping Jennifer with Adan.

There is a place somewhere between the rush of adrenaline and the onset of panic when one thinks and/or does crazy things.

When they all got up to make their escape, Eugene left everything behind, including his jacket and one shoe he'd removed. KC on the other hand, scooped up all her belongings, coat, purse, even both pink sandals she had kicked off.

Struggling along the sidewalk behind the Cineplex, Eugene thought KC was right behind him...she wasn't. Much to his horror, she was still standing by the exit, having dropped her sandals. She was franticly digging through her purse.

He limped back to her, "What are you doing?"

"Looking for my car keys."

Either on her own, or with her future husband's prompting, perhaps both, KC came to her senses and they both followed the other three along the back of the building and around the corner.

Taking inventory, Jennifer realized she had been hit twice in the head with shrapnel from the plastic seat in front of her. Seven days after the shooting, KC plucked a bullet fragment out of her own back.

Painful to look at is an aerial photo of the killer's car, doors open, several officers, including at least three ATF personnel, milled around the exit and bloody footprints led from it...all the blood was from Adan and Eugene. In the upper left corner, more blood, the killer's abandoned AR15 and a pair of pink sandals.

Since they knew I was a Vietnam Vet, someone from our church gave me the paperback, *Five Women I Love*, by Bob Hope about his USO tours of Vietnam . In one of the photos, I saw Hope and Joey Heatherton on stage. In the background, standing at parade rest, wearing full MP kit, is my buddy, Jack Garchow.

The timing was perfect. As I grew in my faith, I began to realize increasingly how big a part the Lord played in my life...in all of life. Jack was another one who made it home but seeing his photo after so many years triggered my memory of the MPs I'm aware of who didn't.

- The three killed in the Victoria Hotel attack which included Patrick Brems from my academy cycle (as with McKenna Gate, there is now a Brems barracks in Fort Gordon).

- The accidental drowning of the kid we called Alphabet from my platoon at the academy.

- The 27 killed during Tet, mostly from the 716th, the company that replaced mine in Saigon.

Recently, thanks to Jim Stewart's site, *Military Police of the Vietnam War*, I've seen several photos of the truck on which those 16 MPs were killed on their way to the Tan Son Nhut Airbase during Tet. The truck may have been towed to a safe area and the bodies removed, but the color photographs are at once heartbreaking and horrifying.

- Sgt. Eugene Cox and PFC James Workman, also from the 716th, shot to death in a bar after being summoned because of an altercation involving a GI. Something I did, dozens of times.

- From my own Company, the 560th, PFC Peter Feierabend in a theater attack in Saigon.

- PFCs John Shea and Hank Holguin as door gunners out of Vinh Long.

- Cpl. Terry Woodroffe and SP4 Mark Wittbracht, in vehicular accidents.

- In my own 2nd platoon right there in Vung Tau, the two deaths I touched on briefly earlier in this Memoir: SP4 Richard Whitehouse, drowned after an incident on a PBR while patrolling Vung Tau harbor, and PFC Larry Dupre, knifed to death in an alley in town. Was it the one I was always patrolling off Hoang Dieu street adjacent to the Rex?

All I suffered was a permanent 60% hearing loss in my right ear and 40% in my left. Due to exposure to M14, M16, M79 grenade launchers, percussion grenades, .50 caliber and M60 machine guns and of course my .45. All without ear protection. The incident in the cleaning room being the most significant. The thought of which always triggers the memory of almost killing Billy Butler. I will never again pick up a .45.

It's all in the combination of timing, location and circumstances, but it's not fate...it's never fate.

There is a plaque sold in most Christian bookstores, by an unknown author that reads: *"Those who leave everything in God's hands will eventually see God's hand in everything."*

A clever play on words, but also true. I began to realize His hand was indeed in everything. All of it. Why He kept me from harm's way, I don't know. Isaiah 55:9, *"For as the heavens are higher than the earth, so are my ways higher than your ways and my thoughts than your thoughts."*

Others who have left everything in God's hands are KC and Eugene Han, their stories go way beyond their *near-death experience.* Indeed, they grew from that experience. They chose to be married on the date of the shooting one year later, wanting to change a horrific memory into one of joy. Eugene has recovered from his wounds with only a slight limp from time-to-time. The Hans now have a beautiful daughter named Yuri which means the "Light of God" in Hebrew and "He Shines" in Spanish.

As for me, my "black and white photograph" has brought back all the memories...both good and bad. Some made me smile, some made me weep but all have helped me grow in my faith. *"It's all part of the journey."*

Somewhere along that journey, I gave up darts since most dart players seemed to have darts in one hand and a beer in the other.

I haven't given up cycling, not yet, not quite. I now have a recumbent trike (two wheels forward). At my age, it's the only way I can maintain speed and distance, mainly because it's like peddling for miles on end in a La-Z-Boy® recliner.

So, as I mount my new steed and ride off into the sunset, once again, like John Wayne in *She Wore a Yellow Ribbon,* I look forward to a new tomorrow and eventually my eternal tomorrows.

"When we've been there 10,000 years,
Bright shining as the sun,
We've no less days to sing God's praise.
Then when we first begun."
--Amazing Grace—

In memorandum:

To all my siblings who have gone before me and didn't really get to know *little brother,*

> "Endings are the saddest part.
> but we had a happy middle
> and a very happy start."

especially to the closest one in age whom I miss a lot, brother Les, I wish you had gotten to read this.

ACKNOWLEDGEMENTS

To Jim Stewart of the 552nd and 560th military police companies whose memoir, *Angel From Vietnam* was the inspiration for my own story and for all my questions he so patiently addressed.

To Dave Cooper of the 720th MPs for his many suggestions and memories of Vung Tau. Dave even scrounged up a 1960's era map of the town.

To my beautiful wife, Sherry, whose patience, encouragement and editing skills have made this memoir possible.

Finally, my sisters-in-law, Pam and Karon, whose proofreading abilities have paid off in spades.

Made in the USA
Coppell, TX
29 December 2021

70399327R00114